Ending Stress

Ending Stress

Know Reality. Find Peace.

A practical guide
to nondual meditation

Eliminating stress, anger,
fear and worry
by becoming more realistic

JONATHAN HARRISON

Copyright © 2014, 2015 Jonathan Harrison

Previously published as "Know Reality. Find Peace."

Edited by Barbara Grant
Designed by Ira Keren

Cover image Shutterstock: Migelito, Hammett79

Email jonathan@simplymeditate.org
Website https://endingstress.org

ISBN-13: 978-1-5009-0102-8
ISBN-10: 1-5009-0102-4

"Liberation from stress
is achieved by realizing
the true nature of things
and the way they exist."
- Buddha

"The greatest good
is a peaceful mind."
- Atisha

Contents

Foreword to the second edition 1

Foreword 5

About this guide 7

Part 1. Understanding 9

1. Stress and its elimination 11
2. Practical issues 23
3. Discovering what is real and what is not 29
4. Eliminating worry about non-problems 37
5. Overcoming anxiety, hope and fear 45
6. Removing frustration and anger 51
7. Finding comfort by eliminating fixations 59
8. Minimizing the effect of pain 65
9. Letting your expectations adapt to reality 69
10. Improving your decisions and avoiding guilt 75
11. Respecting your thoughts without believing them 83
12. Cultivating beneficial relationships 89
13. Generating immunity to praise and criticism 97
14. Achieving total freedom 101

15.	Fulfilling yourself now	105
16.	Effortless survival	109
17.	Exploiting everything	113
18.	Discovering that there is nothing special to do	117

PART 2. REALIZING 123

19.	About meditation	125
20.	Families of Buddhist meditation	129
21.	Stages of meditation	133

FREQUENTLY ASKED QUESTIONS 145

ACKNOWLEDGEMENTS 159

REFERENCES 161

AFTERWORD 163

A REMINDER 165

RESOURCES 167

HOW TO CONTACT ME 169

INDEX 170

Foreword to the Second Edition

Lightening the Load

There is a famous sharp Zen story, which goes like this. A seeker wandered far and wide in search of liberation. Eventually after much difficulty he heard about an enlightened master who might help him. He found the master who was a simple old man walking along a path carrying a large bundle of firewood on his back. He asked the master: 'How do I become completely free?' The master looked at him and then put down the bundle he was carrying. He didn't say a word. After some time the seeker asked impatiently: 'Is that it? Then what?' The master picked up his bundle, hoisted it on his back and continued on his way.

We all wish we could put down the loads we are carrying through life. There are internal loads such as anxiety, lack of joy, restlessness or a judgmental mind. Or they seem to be external loads such as not getting what we want or relationship issues or our bodies that seem to betray us. But they are actually also in our minds, for life is constantly changing and how we face change is entirely up to us. The loads seem quite stuck to us. Indeed they have become part of us. They don't get dropped by wishing to be load free, nor by thinking about them, nor by imagining them to have dropped, nor by denying them. We need something else. As Einstein once said: 'You can't solve problems with the same mind that created them.' We need some help because the stress is so much integral to our life that, trying to clean it, we find we are always washing ourselves with dirty water.

This is where meditation and spiritual practices are important. There is no doubt that the Zen master could put his burden down so absolutely only after much Zen practice. Something needs to be shifted at the deepest level, how we are with ourselves, with our experiences and with the world, moment by moment. And then something extraordinary happens. We discover that our very nature is peaceful, joyful and connected, but we could not see it because it was obscured by the beliefs, stories, memories, narratives and habits that filled our consciousness with clouds. Once the clouds can be seen as unreal and not solid, the sun shines out. And in its light our view of reality expands way beyond the boundaries that we thought were the world.

Learning meditation is not easy and it is not difficult. It is helpful if there is some good teaching to set us on the right path. This is where this book comes in. Jonathan Harrison has written a wonderful manual which is remarkable in its directness, simplicity, and sharpness. It offers very concise instructions not only on meditation but also on different ways of viewing ourselves and the world. They go together. The text is similar to what's called the 'pith instructions' in Tibetan texts: short, deep and pithy, guiding on method but also pointing out the kinds of experiences and shifts in view to be noticed on the way. Meditation is not in the end just a technique, but another way of knowing, of being a conscious human being—a knowing that is clear, free, unconditioned and boundless. That is why questioning and inquiry are so important along with meditation in the whole range of Buddhist paths. This book does it very well—opening up and questioning those things that we always took to be real, what we assumed were facts. In particular how we shape what we see and know, according to what we want to see and know. Through the exercises and the concise clear text of this book, the world as we usually know it, that gives us stress and pain, is thrown open and deconstructed. And we are guided to the clarity and peace of our true being.

Dr. Stephen Fulder

Foreword

Even though the vision of nondual reality exists in most religions and spiritual traditions it is still unknown to most practitioners. Even within Buddhism where nonduality is the foundational perspective of all Mahayana traditions, many practitioners are unaware that Mahayana wisdom is thoroughly nondual. The term "nondual" is used repeatedly in ancient sutras and texts. I have been aware for some years of the importance of re-emphasizing the nondual source and power of the Buddha's message of freedom and in reaffirming Buddhism as "the ultimate medicine" as expressed so clearly in the four noble truths.

The challenge that has confronted Buddhists for millennia is how to clearly and purely transmit a teaching that is ultimately contentless. Although this stainless state is clearly central in all traditions that rely on the Prajnaparamita, it isn't always a simple task to go beyond the knowing mind and presence the inconceivable.

For these reasons I welcome this guide by Jonathan Harrison. The guide offers a lucid introduction to the ultimate state and outlines clear practices to realization. Jonathan has distilled the essence of nondual approaches to well-being and ultimate fulfillment. Jonathan's analysis of the dualistic mind that produces all our suffering is compelling and I delight in the way he continually points us back to the inherent inner wisdom that is at the core of every conscious being.

He writes with full recognition that the present moment is always the most precious moment in our existence, because it's the only moment in which we can reach our fundamental, primordial nature. Jonathan has created a guide that walks you along the path to nondual awareness, with incredible precision and efficiency, through a set of simple practices. He doesn't waste of moment of your time. While recognizing that ultimately "there is nothing to do," Jonathan provides a set of subtle exercises that dissolve in their very performance, thereby providing gateways into the gateless state of ever-present awareness. He also answers the central questions that arise in nondual work without giving you yet more to ponder and think about. His answers let our minds come to rest in the place of great ease and expansiveness.

This guide gives you everything you need to clearly presence the subtle, yet self-evident state of nondual awareness. I trust that Jonathan's earnest endeavors and the deep wisdom he presents in this guide will be widely appreciated. May the nondual wisdom he reveals find a place in your heart, and may this guide be a companion that you can refer to again and again on your path to discovering lasting peace and unconditional happiness.

Dr. Peter Fenner, Creator of Radiant Mind © and Natural Awakening Trainings

ABOUT THIS GUIDE

I have written this guide to show you the practical application of traditions of nondual[1] wisdom that offer you the possibility of freedom from stress.

The chapters lead you, by stages, from normal thinking, which generates conflict and stress, to a more realistic appreciation of yourself and the world, where the mechanism that generates conflict and stress is absent.

The guide first shows you how to become free of mental disturbance, such as anger, fear, worry and anxiety, in everyday situations. It continues naturally towards the calm and stillness present in the space of natural awareness which emerges spontaneously as the expression of your deepening appreciation of the nature of reality.

You may notice the concepts and language in the guide becoming less structured as you read on, expressing the gentle dissolving of your absolute belief in what you think, accompanied by reduced stress, less effort and more comfort.

The second section of this guide describes a simple seven-stage graded meditation path.

---

[1] Nondual: the view that things appear distinct while not being separate. In this guide, the term 'nondual teachings' refers to the Dzogchen, Mahamudra, Zen, Advaita and Tao wisdom traditions.

In addition there are specific meditation suggestions at the end of each chapter to help you internalize the particular insights of that chapter.

I hope this guide will help you to live more realistically, free from conflict and stress and to experience life in peace and joy.

PART 1. UNDERSTANDING

1. STRESS AND ITS ELIMINATION

Understanding and removing stress

"I teach one thing and one only: stress and the end of stress."
- Buddha

THE NATURE OF STRESS

==Mental stress results from wanting reality to be different from what it is.==

It is self-evident that you prefer to be calm and avoid stress. In order to achieve this, it is enough for you to fully realize three things:

What happens, happens; nothing else happens.

Reality, what actually happens, cannot possibly be different from what it is.

All apparent alternatives to what is happening are imagined, thoughts only.

Common examples of thoughts that cause stress are wishing you were younger or healthier or had more money. So are wishing you had not failed a test or did not get into your car only to find you have a flat tire.

Throughout life you may experience or suffer various expressions of stress including anger, anxiety, disappointment, discontent, dissatisfaction, dread, envy, fear, frustration, guilt, humiliation, impatience, insult, misery, mistrust, regret, tension and worry.

Stress seems to be an inescapable part of life. It causes trouble both for you and people around you. So what causes stress and how can you stop it?

How stress is created

In order to see how stress is created, you need to understand three things:

> the way you think about things;
>
> the way things really are;
>
> the results of confusing these.

The way you think about things

The Sutralamkara[2] states:

> Know that nothing exists apart from the mind;
> Realize the mind itself is devoid of true reality.

---

[2] Sutralamkara: major work of Buddhist philosophy.

As a human being you see things in terms of your opinions and concepts which appear to split the world into so-called dualistic[3] structures (from the Latin word duo meaning two), for example:

> **Beautiful (or ugly)**: there is no absolute standard and opinions vary widely. Real people and things are neither inherently beautiful nor ugly. A common man sees a beautiful woman as a temptation. A monk sees her as a distraction. A hungry leopard sees her as steak. In fact she is just what she is.
>
> *Beautiful and ugly are opinions, not facts.*
>
> **Religious (or secular)**: A Buddhist, for example, does not conveniently fit into either category. Buddhism is neither a religion nor a non-religion. Some philosophers relate to Buddhism as an atheistic religion. The Dalai Lama[4] calls Buddhism the science of the mind.
>
> *Religious and secular are opinions, not real.*

Your own mental structures consisting of your particular set of opinions and concepts is the result of many factors including your genetic makeup, parental upbringing, social and cultural environments and the way you have perceived, internalized and acted on your experiences. These mental structures develop and change throughout your life. The world as you see it is largely a reflection of your mental history.

---

[3] Dualistic: concepts, the view of things as "this" or "that."
[4] Dalai Lama (the 14th Dalai Lama, Tenzin Gyatso, b. 1935): spiritual leader of Tibet.

Although your thoughts and structures may be of academic interest to a psychologist or neuroscientist, their main functions for you are in organizing your life and as a source of creativity. But just as you do not assume the factual correctness or incorrectness of a novel, symphony or painting, why assume that what you think is true or false? What you think is an original creation of your mind.

You are so used to talking in ideas that you rarely if ever question whether these ideas actually refer to anything real. In fact, it is impossible to think "about something." Thoughts occur, that is all. You do not automatically believe others' thoughts, so why blindly believe your own?

There are three ways of understanding and misunderstanding your thoughts:

> **Thoughts** you see as plain thoughts, coming and going, are harmless neurological processes in and of themselves. They cause no trouble.
>
> **Opinions**, thoughts you believe, tend to cause stress because they often appear to you to clash with reality.
>
> **Beliefs**, opinions you hold absolutely, can cause even more trouble when you defend them with force, mistaking them for facts.

Political and religious beliefs continue to cause much conflict and war in the world.

 ## THE WAY THINGS REALLY ARE

Reality, the world as it is, is neither inherently split (dualistic), nor unified, neither structured nor unstructured. It just is.

This is so simple that most people do not understand it.

THE RESULTS OF CONFUSING YOUR THOUGHTS WITH REALITY

To be real, things must exist regardless of what you think. When you think without checking whether your thoughts refer to anything real, they can lead you absolutely anywhere. There are no limits since your mind is unlimited, unlike reality which is restricted to what actually happens.

Although you can plan now for an imagined desired future, you cannot change what is happening now because it is already happening. You can also not change the future because the future is expectations, imagined and non-existent.

Confusing thoughts with reality creates stress by tempting you to believe in alternative illusory realities, to want things different from what they are, and to fail to understand why this is not working for you. The resulting problems and conflicts can give rise to stress. For example:

> **Your plans may fail.** Since your emotions, and so your actions, stem from what you think is happening, but you necessarily act in the real world, the results of your actions may be very different from what you planned.
>
> **The world may appear to be "broken."** As long as you identify with your opinions, you naïvely judge the world as right or wrong according to how well it matches your opinions and expectations, rather than more sensibly judging the validity of your opinions and expectations by how well they match events. Reality always wins!

People may respond negatively to your behavior when it is inappropriate to what is happening. This can negatively impact your relationships, particularly close ones.

Remember that everything in this guide is **my** opinion, so be careful neither to accept nor reject any of it. Check out everything very carefully for yourself. But remember that your own conclusions are also thoughts, even while they continue to influence your behavior.

This is also an opinion.

So is this...

Ending stress

Although things change all the time, there is no need, or indeed possibility, for you to change anything, merely to grasp deeply how things really work. If you consider carefully, it becomes clear that the past has gone, is unalterable, the future is non-existent except as your present expectations, and "now" is already here with you.

You then realize that change is no more than a philosophical idea. Without your memory (also a mental process) it is impossible to even think of change. Within this realization, true rest occurs naturally even during intense activity. This is non-meditation, natural meditation or "resting in natural awareness" as Longchen Rabjam[5] put it.

By recognizing the nature of reality you are able to live, love and benefit yourself and others more easily, as you no longer experience the frustration of trying to grasp at imagined parts of your experience or trying to remove them.

DISSOLVING THE ILLUSION

It is not easy to grasp that the same thoughts that comprise your knowledge and enable you to function in society do not actually refer to anything real, even though they may work reasonably well quite a lot of the time. But the skill to know the difference is essential for your peace of mind.

Art students are taught this skill when learning how to draw and paint. Art teachers instruct students to draw what their eyes see, not what they think is there. They constantly remind students not to draw and paint from a memory of "what a banana looks like" but rather to observe the specific banana in the still-life fruit arrangement in front of them.

As you increasingly understand that your thoughts do not refer to reality:

You become calmer regardless of how things work out.

---

[5] Lonchen Rabjam (also Longchenpa, 1308–1364): Dzogchen master and major teacher of the Nyingma school of Tibetan Buddhism.

You respect your thoughts that create your imagined world, but as thoughts only.

Things cease to surprise or upset you. You just deal with things as best you can as they happen.

Past childhood and adult difficulties, abuse and trauma cause you less trouble, as they increasingly appear as painful memories rather than reality.

Your mind becomes less capable of creating conflict and stress. The real world as it is can never be in conflict with anything else because there is nothing else with which it can be in conflict.

You become more responsible. Your emotional responses and actions become increasingly relevant to what is happening. Your self-confidence grows. People trust you more. Your relationships are easier and more mutually beneficial. These are powerful sources of wellbeing.

There is an absence of that familiar feeling that something is wrong.

Life becomes easier and more comfortable.

Dissolving your illusion—seeing yourself and the world more realistically—ultimately involves nothing more than resting in natural awareness. Two supporting activities can be useful while this state is repeatedly introduced to you and gradually becomes familiar, ultimately your second nature:

Study: explanations and conversations with teachers and like-minded friends that help you clarify what is real and, more importantly, what is not.

Meditation: experiential activities designed to calm your mind and help you discover the true nature of both yourself and the world.

Study

Ultimately, it is enough to appreciate deeply that what happens, happens and that nothing else ever happens.

This sounds so trivial that it may seem there is really nothing to learn. But to fully appreciate this simple fact may take considerable time, effort and resources. There are many ways to misunderstand it. Although not complex, it is both subtle and elusive.

Are the study and practice actually essential or redundant? Nagarjuna,[6] the first century founder of the Mahayana Buddhism[7] tradition, might have said, "They are neither essential nor non-essential, nor both, nor neither." This work is peppered with apparent paradoxes that melt away as you examine them more closely.

Meditation

Meditation is being awake, aware of what is actually happening. When the Buddha was asked, following his enlightenment, "Are you a god or a man?" he answered, "I am awake."

---

[6] Nagarjuna (c. 150–250): major Buddhist teacher and philosopher, founded the Madhyamaka school of Mahayana Buddhism together with his student Aryadeva.
[7] Mahayana Buddhism: one of the two main existing branches of Buddhism, the other being Theravada.

When you are fully awake, you discover your unconditioned mental space, in which problems cannot exist.

There is a simple meditation at the end of each chapter and a graded meditation path in a separate section at the end of the guide.

THE FOUR ESSENTIAL PROCESSES

Release from stress happens through four processes, although not necessarily in this order:

>**You are introduced to your real nature** and the nature of the world, which ultimately turn out to be the same. This usually requires a teacher. The introduction may be required many times, as you will regularly forget.
>
>**You clearly recognize** and identify your true nature and the nature of the world when they are pointed out to you.
>
>**You become familiar** with this state of recognition; this is usually achieved by meditation.
>
>**You recognize the truth** of this insight in everyday life, until every event becomes more fuel for the process, which naturally develops and stabilizes.

This summary is not essentially different from the three essential points of Garab Dorje:[8]

---

[8] Garab Dorje (c. 55 C.E.): the semi-historical first human teacher of Dzogchen, the Tibetan Great Perfection teachings.

You are introduced to the nature of mind.

You grasp this with total conviction.

You proceed confidently to the result.

[Handwritten margin notes: Recognize / Decide / Liberate / Let in / Let be / Let go]

PARADOXES ON THE WAY

The only thing to learn is that there is nothing to learn

The aim of meditation is to discover that meditation is superfluous

There are surprises on the way. The more you observe reality, the more things you thought were real turn out to be thoughts. There is no need for you to make an effort to be different from what you are now or even to try to stop making this effort. This is because it is impossible. You change all the time anyway, both mentally and physically, but although you are changing, that does not necessarily mean there is anybody doing the changing.

Although you may say "I will change myself," on closer examination it is unclear what this "I" refers to in any tangible sense. It is similar to watching rain fall without needing to invent someone who is actually moving the rain down. The rain is a natural consequence of atmospheric conditions. Similarly, you change constantly as the result of the dynamic nature of your body and mind and the influence of your surroundings on you.

Some people may say that God causes it all, however, since most theistic religions emphasize that God is ineffable and has no attributes, this statement is recognized by those religions as actually meaningless at deeper levels of religious and spiritual understanding.

MEDITATION

Sit quietly in a comfortable place.

Listen to the sounds

Notice your thoughts which identify individual sounds as cars, people and other things.

The sounds come and go.

The thoughts come and go.

Listen to the sounds and observe the thoughts.

You are the witness.

There is nothing special for you to do.

This is meditation, resting in natural awareness, awake.

2. PRACTICAL ISSUES

Without application, theory is just talk

"I maintain that Truth is a pathless land, and you cannot approach it by any path whatsoever, by any religion, by any sect."
- *Krishnamurti*[9]

THE PATH

Before it becomes clear that, ultimately, no path to peace of mind exists, it may be convenient to refer to one to get going. As with geographical navigation, your path to where you want to be depends on your starting point. You may be reading this guide because you:

> Are fed up with the difficulties of life and wish to live more comfortably;

---

[9] Jiddu Krishnamurti (1895–1986): major writer and speaker on philosophical and spiritual issues.

- Are facing illness, a crisis in your family or other personal relationships, or your job;
- Have already studied one or more meditative approaches with incomplete satisfaction;
- Need to change your life, stop smoking, lose weight or take other apparently difficult actions;
- Need to make a critical decision or choice;
- Are frightened about death;
- Wish to help not only yourself but also others to be free from stress;
- Are a therapist, teacher or your occupation involves listening and responding, and you wish to avail yourself of additional tools in your work.

Spontaneous Awakening

Some people 'get it' alone. The penny drops for them. If you are one of these people, you do not need this guide. Examples of people who 'got it' include the Buddha, but many lesser known people get it alone also. You may not identify them as such but become aware of a quiet feeling of nonjudgmental peace, calm, clarity, openness, listening, love, comfort, and spaciousness in their presence.

Finding a Teacher

You are unlikely to acquire your desired result from books alone. Although you can gain valuable information and inspiration from books, only a realized teacher or friend can help you gain the extremely subtle appreciation of the truth.

You feel something special in the presence of a realized teacher that lends context and deep cognitive and experiential resonance to other, passive, sources of information. All the traditions emphasize the essential role of direct transmission between teacher and student.

This guide is not intended to replace teachers but to be used, together with study with a teacher and regular meditation, as a handbook, to clarify and to act as a reminder.

Depending on your situation, personality, abilities and stage of life, different teachers may be appropriate. If you find a teacher with whom you feel calm, this is a good indication. Do not only listen to your teacher, but carefully observe how he/she behaves with other people.

It is enough to be in the presence of a realized teacher for the teaching to happen. There is nothing specific that you need to do. You will find yourself naturally asking for what you want and the teacher will respond appropriately to your changing needs with love and sensitivity.

If you feel your teacher is ego-centered or guarding his or her own interests, tell them. If you are consistently uncomfortable with the responses, leave and find a teacher who is more suitable for you.

A teacher is in any case a temporary stand-in, reflecting you back to yourself so that you can learn who you are and what the world is. The ultimate teacher is always you and your life.

A Buddhist proverb states "when the student is ready, the teacher appears." This does not mean that a genie guru materializes out of a spiritual bottle. It means that every moment of life can become an opportunity to increase your awareness provided you are open to it. In this sense you create your teachers.

The Role of the Teacher

The role of a teacher in this context is not to know.

At this moment you probably know quite a lot, and this so-called knowledge, without your realizing it, causes you trouble since it creates expectations that regularly seem to clash with what actually happens.

If your work together is fruitful, you will gradually know less and less. Ultimately, you may also know nothing. At this point, one of the things you will not know is who the teacher is and who the student is. This point will become naturally clear to both you and your teacher.

At this point you can continue alone, on your own path which is unique. It is always beneficial to be in the company of like-minded people for mutual love, support and inspiration.

Choosing Private or Group Study

You may prefer to study alone with your teacher or in a group. Both contexts have their value and limitations. Group study is usually less expensive and you may enjoy the support of the other people in the group. Individual study is more intimate and accurate, focusing on your particular needs and exploiting your special background. You can also raise private issues that may be unsuitable for group work.

You can combine these. Gently sense what suits you, and if necessary consult with your teacher. Do not be afraid to change when the situation requires it. A good teacher will help you make changes when necessary.

If you want to realize the truth, you must come close to the source of the truth. That is the teacher. Even your teacher does not know what he/she is teaching and what is learnt. Even when you are fully aware, you will not be able to explain what you have learnt. Eventually you may teach others. You will not know what you are teaching—the teaching happens. The flower and the fire will be inside you and the fragrance and heat can be sensed by anyone close to you.

THE COMPONENTS OF THE WORK

Your work consists of study, meditation and living compassionately, that is with equal concern for all including yourself. These three are complementary. No one or two are adequate.

> **It is not enough to study**—this usually results in dry knowledge, or worse, in the belief that you know.
>
> **It is not enough to practice meditation**—meditation is extremely subtle and most unguided meditation leads to a dead end, frustration and the invalidation of meditation as a tool for eliminating stress.
>
> **The most powerful component is compassion,** unconditional love, kindness. This removes barriers that meditation and study alone are powerless to address. Compassion stems naturally from study and meditation as you realize deeply that you are not separate from everything and everyone else.

Preparation

You may need to do some preliminary work on yourself before commencing your spiritual development. If you are aware of specific disturbing feelings or behavior patterns, a period of Western-style psychotherapy may be in order either before or in parallel with spiritual work. A good teacher will help you to decide where to start, and with what. As the Dalai Lama once said, "Remember, Buddhism is not everything!"

Spiritual work is not medicine. If you are suffering from physical or mental illness, seek medical, dietary, psychiatric or other appropriate advice. You may be able to continue your spiritual work in parallel. Consult both your physician and spiritual teacher if in doubt.

3. Discovering What Is Real and What Is Not

By realizing what is real, and more importantly what is not real, the unreal ceases to disturb you

"The real does not die, the unreal never lived."
- Nisargadatta Maharaj[10]

What You Think and What Is Real

Pain is an unavoidable part of life. Stress is your reaction to this pain, the feeling that this "should not be happening." Whether it should or should not be happening is an opinion, a mental process. Either way, it *is* happening. We could call the pain "primary suffering" and the stress "secondary" (or neurotic) suffering. Often the neurotic component acts as an

---

[10] Nisargadatta Maharaj (1897–1981): Indian spiritual teacher and philosopher of Advaita (Nondualism).

amplifier. Sometimes this secondary suffering is much greater than the primary pain.

Learning to be realistic eliminates secondary suffering, leaving the pain as pure sensation.

So how can you discover what is real and more importantly, what is unreal?

There are three understandings that help you appreciate that your thoughts and concepts do not refer to anything real. Buddhists call them the three seals:

> Everything changes.
>
> Everything is influenced by, and in turn influences other things.
>
> As a result, your concepts do not refer to anything real.

EVERYTHING CHANGES

Although a mountain may seem permanent to you, from the point of view of cosmological history, in the 14 billion years since the Big Bang, your mountain is an infinitesimal flash in time. On the other hand, if mayflies, whose lifespan is from 30 minutes to a day, could think, you would seem permanent to them. Relative to them your lifespan would seem around fifty million years.

Since everything changes, your concepts lack validity, since the world has changed since your mind formed them by abstraction from a few arbitrarily selected details.

Everything is influenced by and influences other things

In reality there seem to be no isolated systems or phenomena. Everything and everyone is influenced by and influences other things. The world can be likened to a seamless fabric of mutual influences. All separations and combinations are arbitrary. The only thing you might say exists is… everything. But not necessarily the way you think about it.

Since there are no separate things, whenever you think about something, your thought cannot refer to anything real.

As a result, your concepts do not refer to anything real

As you begin to appreciate these first two principles, it becomes clear to you that all your thoughts, concepts, opinions and knowledge are empty, meaning that that they do not refer to anything real, but are simply mental constructs.

Reality is everything, but not what you think. This is why witnesses can argue about what they think happened. If they all knew what really happened they would all agree.

The Buddha suggested that there is no need to seek reality; it is enough to discard your opinions.

You can never know whether something is actually happening. What seems to be happening you call your experience.

The real is unknown; the known is unreal.

Mental constructs

Here are some examples of mental constructs. They can be found only as thought processes and do not refer to anything real, much as they initially seem to. Check them carefully for yourself and attempt to find them without using your thoughts:

Identities: I, you, body, mind, individual, group, city, state;

Opinions: attitudes, beliefs, prejudices, concepts, fixations, ideas, perceptions, judgments, values, right, wrong, best, worst, should/should not, must/must not;

Unconscious beliefs: beliefs you do not know you even hold (try to find some);

Relationships: partner, parent, boss, friend, enemy, owner, similar, different, separate, unified;

Situations: what you think is happening;

Time: the past (memories), the future (expectations);

Knowledge: whatever you think or know;

Quantities: one, two, a million;

Defined things: anything in a dictionary;

Structures: anything that has components with relationships between the components.

How many parts can you remove from a bicycle before it ceases to be a bicycle? Can this be discussed or is the number of parts a fact?

If you deal only with reality, what is actually happening, now, at this point, you can find neither structures nor the absence of structures. You cannot examine the structure of a single point.

All boundaries are arbitrary. No one has ever seen a real boundary, one that is independent of thinking. Boundaries can be changed simply by redefining them through individual thinking or by consensus, the name we give to collectively agreed thinking, but reality cannot be changed by thought or agreement.

A bird sitting on a fence separating two sovereign states, on seeing a worm just eats it. It is of no interest to the bird to which state the worm "belongs." The bird does not recognize the existence of sovereign states.

Anything you can define has no real existence.

The real does not need defining, it already is.

THE TWO CENTRAL QUESTIONS

There are two questions you can ask yourself in order to establish firmly in your mind what is real and what is not. These questions should be considered deeply until you are absolutely sure you have the final and absolutely irrefutable answer. Not finding an answer is also an answer. You may consider these fundamental questions for many years, finding new depths of understanding each time.

Who am I?
What is this?

Who am "I"?

When you think or say "I," what exactly do you mean?

Ask yourself, "Who am I, if not who I think I am?"

Whatever answer you find is a thought. If "I" is real, it is not that.

"Then who am I really?"

Can you answer this without resorting to further thoughts? If you can, your answer is nevertheless a thought, so you are not that.

If you cannot, why not?

Consider these points:

> Your body is the name you give to a highly dynamic, fluid collection of material, continually collecting, dispersing and changing its form indefinitely, from long before your birth till long after your death.
>
> Your mind is the name you give to your ever-changing thoughts, emotions and sensations.

If so, does this "I" thing that you believe owns, experiences and controls your body and mind, refer to anything real? Ask yourself,

> "What am I really, if not what I think?"
>
> "What, if anything, actually controls my thoughts? Is there anything real, or are they simply part of a naturally unfolding process?"
>
> "Can I guarantee my next thought, or what I will be thinking in exactly one minute from now?"

Can you reach definite conclusions, independent of your thoughts?

What is This?

Anything you identify is not real. Identification is a thought, based on remembered concepts. If you know what it is, it is not real; knowledge is a collection of thoughts. Try asking yourself, "What is this, if not what I think it is?"

Meditation

Sit comfortably.

Listen to the sounds.

Now listen to the sounds you missed the first time.

Listen to all the sounds.

Notice how the medley of sound changes from moment to moment. The sound of a car going past… you hear it and it passes. A dog barks and the bark is gone. Your breath goes in…and out.

Your memory is of no help in knowing what sound you will hear next.

It all changes. Things come and go.

4. Eliminating Worry About Non-Problems

It is impossible to solve a non-existent problem

"If there is a problem and a solution, there is no need to worry. If there is a problem and no solution there is no point in worrying."
- Shantideva[11]

The Nature of Problems and Worries

You worry when you think that something important in the future will not be the way you want it to be, but do not know how to fix that.

The error is in thinking you need to guarantee the future. When you realize that the future has no real existence, that there is actually nothing whatever that can possibly be

---

[11] Shantideva (c. 685–763): Indian Buddhist scholar at Nalanda University.

guaranteed, the worry stops. You do what you do, and what happens, happens. You may plan now for an imagined future, but it is worthwhile remembering that this so-called future is only a mental picture. When whatever happens actually happens, you will deal with that.

A Zen[12] student asked his teacher, "Master, what is enlightenment?" The master replied, "When hungry, eat. When tired, sleep." You naturally act to get what you want. A thought that immediately converts to a relevant action does not normally constitute a problem you worry about.

When you want something but no obvious course of action occurs to you, or if the necessary action seems impossible, you may perceive a problem. When you need to change or avoid an expected painful or difficult situation, you may see this also as a problem. In these situations you may worry.

Since you do not knowingly worry about an imaginary problem, only real ones, the method is to know the difference. Worry is an expression of confusing real with imaginary problems. In fact, there are no real problems.

Here are some worries people have presented to me in conversations that expose the illusions hidden in thought processes. You may recognize parallels for some of them in your own life:

"My boss wants to talk to me."

---

[12] Zen: school of Mahayana Buddhism originating in China (as Chan) during the sixth century C.E.

"I have too much to do."

"I am waiting for the results of a medical test."

"My son is in a bad relationship."

"The political situation is very worrying."

"My mother is late."

My boss wants to talk to me

Helen: My boss wants to talk to me. I think she is dissatisfied with my work. How can I convince her?
Jonathan: Can you definitely control the outcome of the meeting?
Helen: No.
Jonathan: You do not know what her actual attitude is or how it will develop towards the meeting. In the same way that your own thoughts reflect your historical conditioning, so hers reflect her mental conditioning, neither of which you control or even begin to understand. Both your and her thoughts are responses to things that happen, which are also not within your control or understanding. So there is no possibility of controlling the outcome of a future interaction between the unknown conditioning, dynamics and personal life situations of two people. This is a non-starter.
Helen: So what should I do?
Jonathan: You may prepare material you feel would be helpful. You may talk to someone you feel might influence things positively. You may eat and sleep well before the meeting. As you begin to realize that it is meaningless to talk or even think about determining this future event, the worry evaporates. It is simply not your job to control the future. You think what you think, you do what you do and

what happens, happens. That is all. If you look after your mental health and even use the meeting as a stepping stone for your spiritual and personal development by deepening your appreciation of how things work, it becomes a force for good regardless of the outcome.
Helen: That sounds good. I hope I can apply it.
Jonathan: The application consists in appreciating that there is nothing to apply and no one to apply it.
Helen: *Smiles*

I have too much to do

Mark: I have too much to do. I must finish everything this week.
Jonathan: What will happen if you don't finish everything?
Mark: I must finish it.
Jonathan: I understand. It is important. But what is the worst case?
Mark: The files have to be sent to head office.
Jonathan: What will happen if only some of them go this week?
Mark: They will not be reviewed in time. I have to send them all.
Jonathan: "I must finish," "I have to send them all" are thoughts. In practice you will do what you actually do. If you are committed to more than you can actually manage then you will not do some of the things." There are three stages: (1) make a list, (2) prioritize the list (3) do the first thing on the list. In reality you only ever do one thing at any physical moment.
Mark: I suppose so. But my job is to finish them all.
Jonathan: How many are there to be closed and sent this week? 10? 100? 1,000?
Mark: Seven.

ELIMINATING WORRY ABOUT NON-PROBLEMS

Jonathan: How many files can do realistically do?
Mark: Three or four.
Jonathan: What would happen if they gave you 1,000 to do this week. Would it actually be your job to do all 1,000?
Mark: *Smiles* ... I couldn't do 1,000.
Jonathan So is it your job or not?
Mark: I see what you mean.
Jonathan Is there a possibility of doing more than you actually can?
Mark: No.
Jonathan You will, in any case, do what you can. How about doing what you can, but doing it happily? Is that a possibility?
Mark: *Smiles*

I am waiting for the results of a medical test

Richard: I am waiting for the results of the test.
Jonathan: What is the worst that could happen?
Richard: I don't know.
Jonathan: You do know. Is it frightening?
Richard: Yes.
Jonathan: What is the worst?
Richard: *Silence...* I don't want to think about it.
Jonathan: Do you know the result already?
Richard: It might be cancer.
Jonathan: But do you know that now?
Richard: No.
Jonathan: Is it true that you might have cancer and you might not have cancer?
Richard: Yes
Jonathan: Right now, you are neither aware that you have cancer nor that you don't have cancer. When are the results due?

Richard: Thursday.
Jonathan: On Thursday you may find out you have cancer. Then you will deal with that. On the other hand you may find out you do not have cancer. Then you will deal with that. Right now you cannot deal with either of these because neither exists. Is it clear that it is impossible to solve a non-existent problem?
Richard: Yes.
Jonathan: Is there anything we need to do about it now?
Richard: No.
Jonathan: Is it possible to rest for now, and then deal with whatever situation occurs on Thursday?
Richard: Yes. *Silence*

My son is in a bad relationship

Debbie: My youngest son's wife is being influenced by her mother and causing trouble.
Jonathan: *Silence*
Debbie: I don't know what to do about it.
Jonathan: Is there anything you can do about it?
Debbie: Not really. It worries me.
Jonathan: What would most contribute to helping?
Debbie: He is so stressed, it upsets me.
Jonathan: The more you are a mother to him, the more he feels you understand and do not judge either him or his wife, the more he can gain strength from you and will be more likely to know what to do himself. Do you love him?
Debbie: Yes.
Jonathan: Is that enough?
Debbie: Is there something I can do?
Jonathan: Is there anything you can do about it?
Debbie: No.

Jonathan: If you relax, he will gain from that. Is it possible that love is what he most needs now? Non-judgmental, unconditional love?
Debbie: Yes.
Debbie: *Silence...*
Debbie: How will he manage? I can't tolerate my children unhappy. What do I need to do?
Jonathan: Can you absolutely guarantee that your children will be happy?
Debbie: No.
Jonathan: Is it possible that you will do everything right and they will still not be happy?
Debbie: Yes. I see.
Jonathan: Is it possible that you can make serious mistakes, but your children will survive them and be happy anyway?
Debbie: Yes, I suppose I do not really control it.
Jonathan: Is there anything else we need to do now about this?
Debbie: No, not now.

The political situation is very worrying

Alex: I am worried about this news.
Jonathan: Do you need to do anything about it now?
Alex: No.

My mother is late

Sophie: My mother is very late and I cannot contact her. I don't know what has happened to her.
Jonathan: How late is she?

Sophie: She should have called me from home two hours ago.
Jonathan: Do you want to call the police?
Sophie: Not yet. It is not the first time. Maybe I should go to her house.
Jonathan: Do you want to go now?
Sophie: I'll wait another hour, then go.
Jonathan: Is there anything more to do now?
Sophie: No.
Jonathan: Is it possible to rest comfortably for this hour, keep an eye on the clock, and stay aware of the possibilities? Is that acceptable to you? Is there anything else at the moment?
Sophie: No. *Relaxes*
Jonathan: Shall we do that? Is that acceptable to you or not?
Sophie: Yes, that's ok.

MEDITATION

Sit comfortably.

Consider a problem that occupies or has recently occupied you.

Can you separate it into the real elements, what is actually happening now, and the mental elements, the imaginary structure that creates the problem?

What emotional changes do you experience during this brief investigation?

5. Overcoming Anxiety, Hope and Fear

Even hope involves the anxiety of not getting what you hope for

"Timelessness is beyond the illusion of time. You are too much concerned with past and future. It is all due to your longing to continue, to protect yourself against extinction. But what you call survival is but the survival of a dream."
- Nisargadatta Maharaj

The Search for Security

It is easy to understand that you would like to avoid anxiety and fear, but you probably regard hope as a positive emotion. The problem is that is impossible to hope without an accompanying fear of not getting what you hope for.

Hope and fear both involve the anxiety of uncertainty. You would like to control the future, but do not know how to do so. Things often work out very differently from what you plan.

You naturally and unconsciously seek security by "knowing"—that is by creating mental models, patterns, frameworks or concepts of how things work—what I am, what the world is and what relationships exist between these two apparently separate things.

This is not a problem, provided you fully realize these mental constructs are ideas, magical games of the mind, not reality itself. Your thoughts reflect your mental history, your conditioning, rather than reality. Reality is what actually happens, not what you think happens. When this realization is there, when you are fully aware that you are conditioned, thoughts appear as mental events rather than as information about reality.

The stress, caused by fear, hope and anxiety, stems from not understanding uncertainty. You have good reason to misunderstand uncertainty, having been taught your whole life to try and control the future.

The messages you received from your parents, teachers and society at large involved achieving what you want and what they wanted from you. This probably included a successful career, a suitable partner, material satisfaction and social status.

However, your education in all likelihood did not make clear that you are not in control of these. Many factors influence the future. You do not control, understand or even know about most of them, not even the functioning of your own body and mind, which are products of your genetics, social conditioning and how you have internalized your experiences.

Major social, political and financial changes can totally alter your situation. On a short time scale, your digestion, being at

OVERCOMING ANXIETY, HOPE AND FEAR

the wrong place at the wrong time or the right place at the right time, the weather or even minute-by-minute interactions with people can all dramatically affect things.

The inherent uncertainty of the future, together with your belief that you must control it, provokes anxiety, particularly where the outcome is important to you. Understanding the nature of the future and of uncertainty removes this anxiety. How does this work?

When you look carefully at the future you cannot find it. Look around the room where you are now. Can you find any tangible evidence of the existence of the future? Think of a future event. Can you actually find the event, now, beyond your thoughts, expectations, fears and hopes?

As you examine what you call the future more and more, you find it less and less. The future exists only as expectations and thoughts. You may say you think about the future, but actually you cannot think about the future, you can only think. The thought is happening now. It does not refer to anything real.

Try to find this "future" to which you believe your thought refers. The more you look, the clearer it is that it is not there now. What will happen will happen. Right now you do not know what that is. Whatever you are thinking about is not the future, it is a thought.

Suppose I have had a medical examination for cancer and need to wait three weeks for the biopsy results. The result may be positive, in which case I may face a difficult period of treatment, physical discomfort, impaired functioning, and the knowledge that I am expected to die sooner than I thought. It may be negative in which case there is nothing special I will need to do.

If it is positive, I will find myself dealing with that, if negative, with that. But right now I can deal neither with cancer nor with non-cancer. Neither situation exists right now. One of them will occur, unless of course I die now, in which case both possibilities are academic.

Independently of any result, I can go through three weeks of mental anguish completely unrelated to cancer. This is a total waste of time and energy. An alternative strategy is to live well for now, plan what is relevant and deal with whatever occurs as well as I can when it happens.

In fact it is not clear that there is a better option. What do you think? Only your opinion counts, as that is what motivates you.

Living comfortably with insecurity

The moment you get used to uncertainty, not as a problem but as the very nature of things, life is easier. Living comfortably with uncertainty is a key to comfort, maybe the key. Through study and meditation you progress through three stages of understanding:

> **Knowing**: Initially you know. You operate ignorantly out of your normal conditioned mind. You regard your opinions, beliefs and knowledge as facts. When things work out differently, you feel reality has gone wrong; you experience stress.
>
> **Not knowing**: You begin to realize your knowledge is a collection of thoughts and prejudices and as such is

empty. It refers to nothing. You do not know. This intermediate stage can be anxiety-provoking. You may give up and return to your previous state of knowing, upset each time your knowledge loses its validity. But you may also proceed to the third stage of non-knowing.

Non-knowing: This is the gate to happiness and peace of mind. Neither knowing nor not knowing, neither understanding nor not understanding, you begin to appreciate that you do not know, not because you are stupid or lazy or missing information but because in reality there is nothing to be known. You become aware that your knowledge is an inappropriate tool for appreciating reality. As you access your unconditioned mind, your view of absolute reality unconditioned by your mental history, anxiety evaporates and you experience total peace.

This experience of your unconditioned mind is in itself neither conditioned nor unconditioned. There is no anxiety associated with this state, since your unconditioned mind cannot be gained or lost as it is not a thing. You naturally move in and out of this state but as long as it is clear that it is not you that is doing it, you stay relaxed, enjoying the trip.

Your mind and body continue to operate from your conditioned mind for the practical organization of life. You continue to react and behave according to your expectations or so-called "knowledge," but now with the awareness that your knowledge does not reflect reality. This no longer constitutes a problem or failure. By appreciating the true nature of things, you achieve deep, robust serenity which is capable of withstanding even the inevitable difficult life circumstances which you experience from birth through death including these events also.

Meditation

Sit comfortably.

Think of what you plan to do tomorrow.

Think of some of the things on which your plan depends. Do you completely control all of them?

Can you absolutely guarantee your plan will work out exactly?

Can you plan what you will do in all the possible different circumstances that may alter your plans? Is that possible or not?

Can you rest comfortably knowing that this uncertainty is not your failure but rather the nature of things?

Reach any conclusions you can.

6. REMOVING FRUSTRATION AND ANGER

Reality, 'what is,' cannot be judged against anything else because there is nothing else

"What does reality care what I think about it."
- David Bohm[13]

THREE ERRONEOUS BELIEFS

A young woman told me recently that her husband, a professional, regularly comes home late in the evening, leaving her alone to feed and bath her five children and put them to bed. Despite many discussions and arguments over the years the problem persisted. She called him a father in name only and asked me how to get rid of her anger.

---

[13] David Bohm (1917–1992): American-born British quantum physicist, held discussions with Krishnamurti regarding fundamental issues of the nature of truth and reality.

Anger arises due to three erroneous beliefs or errors of perception:

> You believe you know what is happening.
>
> You believe you know what should be happening.
>
> You believe these two should be identical.

The more clearly you understand these points, the less anger arises in your life.

YOU BELIEVE YOU KNOW WHAT IS HAPPENING

You do not know what is actually happening. You know only what you think is happening. What is happening is far more complex than you can ever imagine.

Are you *really* aware of every single cause and effect in space and time involved in any situation? Our thoughts are superficial, outdated and simplistic compared to reality, with its seemingly infinite web of causes and effects. What you think is happening is just that—a thought, a mental picture.

YOU BELIEVE YOU KNOW WHAT SHOULD BE HAPPENING

How do you really know what should be happening? "What should be happening" is a value, an opinion. It may be your personal opinion or a widely held convention such as "killing is wrong." Nevertheless, what should be happening is an idea. Reality is what actually happens. Can you see the difference?

You Believe These Two Should Be Identical

What basis do you have for believing the world should operate according to your thoughts, moment by moment? Your thoughts are also part of the world, part of the seemingly infinite web of influences.

You were educated to believe your job is to get what you want. Maybe nobody added that this is not within your control to guarantee. Sometimes you get what you want, sometimes you do not. You may even get something you neither wanted nor expected. Things happen the way they happen, depending on many factors of which you have neither knowledge nor understanding.

When looked at closely, this belief is without foundation. Has everything in life gone exactly your way so far? Can you absolutely guarantee the future, even your next breath?

As you become used to the inevitable gaps between what you want and what is, not as problems but simply the way things are, life is easier. The gaps do not indicate that something is wrong, rather that your expectations are not adequately tuned to reality. They never are, as you have no way of expecting the future. You appreciate that any comparison of reality with anything else is impossible. You cannot compare reality, what is, with anything else because there is nothing else to compare it with.

Anger depends on your judgment that a situation is incorrect. All judgment depends on comparison. You cannot judge a person or situation on its own, without having a standard against which to compare.

When you criticize or judge yourself, you compare what you do (or think or feel) to what you think you should do (or think or feel). The same is true when you judge others.

If your colleague is late to a meeting and does not tell you, you may think that this is the wrong way to behave, a reasonable thought, but which nevertheless depends on you knowing the right way to behave.

There are social conventions—people should be considerate, polite and so on. This is all true in conventional terms, the way society is organized, and presents no problem, but nevertheless standards are ultimately no more than collective thoughts. You cannot establish their truth or falsehood democratically. Many societies are racist, but that does not give racism absolute validity.

Standards and laws are not the way people behave but the way people think they should behave. What is "standard" or "law" in one place may be regarded as non-standard or illegal in other places. When you think things should be a certain way, you are merely attempting to impose your opinions on reality, a non-starter.

Eliminating the Errors of Perception that Enable Anger to Occur

If you invert laws, social conventions or religious laws you find out how people really behave. There is a law that you should stop at a red traffic light, but people do sometimes go through red lights. I remember doing it late one night when coming home tired from some event. My wife was shocked. I was shocked. Nevertheless, it happened.

There is a law that you should not appropriate other people's property. But if you watch babies eating together, they take whatever they want from each other's plates. They need training to fit in with society. That is why there are laws and conventions.

But these laws and conventions are not the way people actually behave. No country or religion has a law that you must breathe. It would be redundant, ridiculous. So laws, rules, conventions and standards show us how things do not happen. If things happened naturally according to the rule, no one would have bothered to create that rule.

When you realize this, it becomes clear there are two aspects to laws. One is practical, enforcing them to the extent possible to order society. For this there are police, laws, courts and prisons.

The other is your vital appreciation that the world, you and other people and events do not in practice necessarily work according to these standards. This protects your mental health. Then, instead of getting angry when there is a difference, you are more likely to use that energy to work to improve things.

There is a public debate in many countries regarding law enforcement. Some people get very angry about crimes, take a punitive approach and want criminals to pay heavily. Others are more liberal, citing a criminal's history, maybe a broken home or abuse and claim these factors should be taken into account. The first group may accuse the second of siding with the criminal instead of the victim.

From the nondual (nonconceptual) point of view there is no real conflict. It is sometimes necessary to put someone in prison because they are a danger to society and need isolating, or to deter others from similar acts. These are practical considerations. But it is possible to do this either with or without anger.

When you act without anger you achieve two things. First, you usually act more relevantly. Anger confuses you. Secondly you do yourself less harm. Repeated anger wastes huge amounts of your energy, creates stress and over time can affect your health.

The Dalai Lama suggested we separate the actor from the action. You can oppose inappropriate behavior without attributing the action solely to any one person.

Both you and the criminal are products of genetics, upbringing, culture, education and experience. Had those been different, you would both be different. You did not ask for your particular personality or specific behavior traits; rather you may have found you have to live with them as best you can.

The Buddhists tell a story of a man who received a blow from a stick in a crowd and started to curse the stick. Someone said to him, "Why do you curse the stick? It does not act on its own. Curse the hand that holds the stick." The man agreed and started to curse the hand. They said to him, "Why curse the hand? It does not act on its own. Curse the man the hand belongs to." He agreed and began to curse the man. They said to him, "Why curse the man? He does not act on his own. Curse all the factors that have brought him to this action."

It is enough to realize deeply that you cannot identify a single point of cause for anything that happens because everything influences and is influenced by other things. It is like mistaking the tip of the iceberg for the whole iceberg. You do not know how the world really works, nor can you begin to fathom the innumerable influences things have on other things.

You can begin to appreciate this through meditation. Notice something happening, and try to establish the absolute ultimate cause for it. Repeated failures drive home the impossibility of doing this. At this point you find yourself incapable of judging or criticizing yourself or others. Instead you quietly work to improve things. Life is easier, more comfortable and more effective.

MEDITATION

Sit comfortably.

Recall a recent situation that angered or frustrated you.

Identify as clearly as you can within the situation:

> *What happened, other than what you think happened (your opinion);*
>
> *What should have happened (another opinion);*
>
> *Why these were different (a third opinion).*

Recall the feeling of anger or frustration.

What really happened, if not what you think happened?

What is your new emotional response to the situation?

What really happened, if not even that?

What is your new emotional response to the situation?

7. FINDING COMFORT BY ELIMINATING FIXATIONS

> By observing your gross, subtle and very subtle thoughts, they become naturally transparent and cease to disturb you

"The dissolving of objects and easing of fixations is peace."
- Nagarjuna

BECOMING AWARE OF OUR THOUGHT PATTERNS

A woman complained to me that her husband was domineering, a control freak, and put up such a fight if he did not get his way that it was not worth opposing him. She suffered greatly in the marriage. He fought with her incessantly; he fought with his sisters and spent much of his spare time in litigation against his ex-wife over custody of their child. She was scared of family meetings and of never-ending meetings with lawyers, through which she supported him but also tried to mollify him.

When we examined things, it turned out that her boss at work was similar, and so was her previous husband. It transpired that her father had also been very controlling. When I asked her if she would like a better partner, a gentle, relating, listening husband she immediately replied, "No, I need a strong man." Her mind had been conditioned from, or even before birth. This was the way that men and women were. Gradually she began to see that these men were in effect all actors in a play scripted by her mind without consulting her.

You are inexorably attracted to known situations. This is a result of trying to avoid uncertainty even when the price is very high. Some beaten women return time and time again to their partners claiming they love them, sometime at the risk of life.

But as you become more realistic you find you gradually stop deceiving yourself. You recognize your inner thought patterns as such and cease to be surprised by your repeated responses to similar situations.

It is a bit like baking cookie men. If you look at the tray of cookies and get angry that they all look like little men, this is crazy. If you notice that the shape of your dough cutter is a little man, it is obvious that you will continue making little men as long as you use this cutter.

You can often see hints of other people's constructs, patterns and fixations but it is very difficult to discover your own, since you have long rationalized them out of conscious awareness and your problems seem to have external causes.

In order to have a chance of discovering your own fixations, you need to be non-judgmental about yourself, otherwise you will frighten yourself off. This non-judgmental attitude arises naturally as a result of appreciating who you really are. Then issues of control, guilt and self-criticism do not arise.

The Three Levels of Thoughts

The Tibetan essence traditions of Dzogchen[14] and Mahamudra[15] distinguish three levels of thoughts: gross, subtle and very subtle.

Gross thoughts are those you normally regard as thoughts, such as, "Where did I leave my keys?"

Subtle thoughts are your moment-by-moment mental sensations that arise in response to sensory information. These have not collected themselves into gross thoughts and flicker in the background without your normally noticing them at all.

Very subtle thoughts comprise your basic belief system, your unconscious memory or conditioning which guide your other thought patterns.

You are usually unaware of even many gross thoughts as they occur. Although you may think, "Where did I leave my keys?" you would probably be occupied with finding them, but without clearly perceiving that a thought event had occurred. As your mind or brain creates thoughts and you

---

[14] Dzogchen (Atiyoga or "Great Perfection"): the natural, primordial state or natural condition of the mind, and a body of teachings and meditation practices aimed at realizing that condition; a central teaching of the Tibetan Nyingma school also practiced by adherents of other Tibetan Buddhist sects. According to its followers, Dzogchen is the highest and most rapid path to full awakening.

[15] Mahamudra: refers to experiencing reality; the culmination of practices of the New Translation schools of Tibetan Buddhism (the second wave of translators of Indian texts in the 11th century).

unconsciously identify with them without realizing you believe them, they create an illusory world that seems real to you. That is why you get upset when the real world works differently. You cannot understand it.

As you use special insight meditation, you begin to watch your gross thoughts more closely and become used to seeing them as you see any other event. They happen, but have no particular significance beyond their own occurrence. Your impression is that your gross thoughts naturally give way to a more open, quieter space.

In this quieter space you may begin to notice your subtle thoughts, which manifest like flickering fireflies. As you watch your subtle thoughts the way you might watch a firework display, they too quieten and you may become aware of your very subtle thoughts. These are not thoughts in the usual sense, rather your historical patterns, a kind of "map" confining your thoughts to its "streets."

Much like a city exists without a map, but is easier to navigate with one, your subtle thoughts exist without your noticing them. These thoughts are easier to navigate if you have a "map" for them and if you have trained your mind to identify the patterns.

Relaxing in Natural Awareness

As you relax in ever fuller awareness, you react less with extreme emotion to every thought. At this point, while observing your thoughts more dispassionately and with less identification, you naturally become aware of the recurrence of certain thought and emotional patterns.

Instead of judging them as good or bad (also opinions or thoughts) you become accustomed to them. You begin to recognize that in certain situations you react certain ways. This is your conditioning.

The more you are aware of your conditioning, the more you are aware that you do not control your thoughts or your world but are at most a witness to their creation; the more these same thoughts lose their power to engender disturbing emotions. You react as you react, but you have less of the feeling that things should not be happening this way.

Things always happen exactly the way they happen. That is all. Life feels easier.

MEDITATION

Keep a notebook in your pocket.

During the week, note down your thoughts and your emotional responses to them.

Mark thoughts and emotions that recur regularly. These constitute conditioned structures.

Look back in your life history and identify the first occasion you remember each thought and accompanying emotion arising.

Go back further and do it again.

And again...

Can you find the absolute origin of each habitual thought construct?

Understand that these constructs create your life situations today and will continue to do so until you are fully cognizant of them and their historical origins.

8. Minimizing the Effect of Pain

Although both physical and mental pain seem to be unavoidable in life, stress—the mental tension of trying to avoid it—is avoidable

Bodily pain is like being struck by an arrow. Mental stress added to the physical pain is like being hit by a second arrow. The wise person stops with the first arrow.
- Buddha

Differentiating between pain and suffering

Physical and mental pain happen. They stem from the nature of our bodies and minds and there is no known way to avoid them completely.

This obvious fact is not so obvious, since you react differently to the presence and absence of pain. When you treat the absence of pain as a standard, the presence of pain creates additional mental stress, the feeling that something is wrong. When you really appreciate that pain is an unavoidable part of your life, you do not regard it as if something was broken. You simply do what can be done to alleviate it.

The feeling that something is wrong, that the world including your body and mind are not working correctly, is a mental creation, the source of mental stress. The world does not work correctly or incorrectly, it works as it does. Correct and incorrect are opinions about the world.

While teaching Buddhist meditation to a group of doctors I suggested that illness and health were concepts, neither of which points to anything real. An argument broke out until one of them said, "Wait a minute, Jonathan is right! We say a person has fever when his temperature goes above 37.5 degrees centigrade. What would happen if the World Health Organization redefined it as 37.4 degrees? Would another hundred thousand people suddenly be ill?"

Nisargadatta Maharaj once said that enlightenment is required only if you are identified with your body, otherwise it is unnecessary. As long as you are identified with your body or your mind, when they exhibit pain you are in pain. When you are not identified with them the pain arises but it does not happen to you. Although this sounds strange, I am speaking from experience.

The Buddha pointed out that you are not your body and not your mind. If you were your body you would not permit it to be ill. If you were your mind you would not permit it to suffer.

I once had a severe ear infection while on holiday, playing on the beach with my children and grandchildren. I felt my head was exploding with pain. It was difficult to focus on and be with the children fully.

I remember clearly as a moment of awareness dawned. The pain was still very much there but it was not happening to me.

It was just there. There was absolutely no tension, but pure sensation.

The day went on; I played with the children and in the evening went to a doctor where I was diagnosed with a serious infection which required two antibiotics and over two weeks to clear.

Stranger still, this is true also for mental pain. I can remember during a difficult financial period being immersed in deep depression. Awareness surfaced and it was as if I had stepped off the railway track—the train of depression came and went but I experienced no damage. The depression appeared as pure experience. There was depression but I was not depressed. I remember saying to myself, "Ah, interesting, so that it what this mind is doing at the moment."

There is a Zen story:

Each morning the monks asked their Zen master, "How are you master?" The master would reply in a loud voice, "Excellent!" One morning a young boy said, "Master, how can you always say 'Excellent!' like that. You are a human being—sometimes you feel good and sometimes bad." The master answered in a gentler voice, "Well, maybe I did not adequately explain. When I feel good, I feel good. When I feel bad, I also feel good."

As you become aware, through study and meditation, of the nature of yourself, who you really are, pain can occur with less involvement and consequent mental stress. This does not mean that meditation is a cure for depression or for physical pain. You may need medical or psychological care, but pain and suffering or mental stress are different phenomena requiring different treatment.

Meditation

Sit somewhere quiet and comfortable.

Watch your breath go in and out.

Watch your bodily sensations

Watch your thoughts come and go.

Watch the watcher?

What is that?

Where is it?

9. Letting Your Expectations Adapt to Reality

This is more successful than demanding that reality adjust itself to your expectations

"Act without expectation."
- *Lao Tzu*[16]

Understanding the Nature of Expectations

Your expectations have nothing to do with the present or future. Nothing has anything to do with the future, since the future has no real existence. Your expectations are the expression of your past and your prejudices.

---

[16] Lao Tzu: a philosopher of ancient China. According to tradition, he lived in the sixth century B.C.E. and wrote the Tao Te Ching, the classic text of Taoism.

We all have expectations. However, a wise person does not expect his or her expectations to be necessarily fulfilled.

Most of the time it does not occur to you to question the validity of your expectations since you are not even aware they exist. In effect you are demanding that reality adjust itself to your ever changing expectations, which is clearly ridiculous. When gaps occur you find yourself reacting through various expressions of tension in different ways according to the particular situation:

> Anger ("You will pay for this!")
>
> Fear ("Help! What's happening to me?")
>
> Anxiety ("I won't manage—what will be?")
>
> Disappointment ("Oh no, I so wanted it.")
>
> Envy ("Why can't I have what she has?")
>
> Guilt ("I feel awful—I know I should have gone to see him.")

The common factor is your ignorance of the existence of your expectations. You are so identified with them it seems you are them. You say, "I expect," rather than, "an expectation seems to be occurring."

Through study and insight meditation you begin to become more aware, moment by moment, of the occurrence of expectations as mental occurrences, not under your control but still seemingly influenced by your history and responding to ever-changing external and internal stimuli. You begin to misidentify from and lose your absolute belief in them.

Your own thoughts and expectations appear to you more and more as events, coming and going like clouds or birds in the sky. Your expectations begin to lose their absolute validity and/or naturally adjust themselves to reality. The gaps begin to dissolve rather than just close. Your disappointment and anger gradually fade in intensity and frequency.

Initially you understand the cause of an emotional upset in retrospect only, some time after the event, if at all. As you continue to study, meditate and internalize the truth of things, this time shortens and eventually disappears.

Ultimately your expectations synchronize themselves with reality as it happens. At this point your expectations cease to upset you. You continue to plan according to your expectations, which reflect your history, but as events unfold your expectations track reality.

You cease to experience a kind of double reality, the real one and the illusory one constructed from your expectations. As soon as something real happens, you no longer need the expectation or mental picture of what you thought would or should happen—you have the real thing.

For practical purposes your expectations still embody your knowledge, but gaps between what you expected and what is happening do not disturb your inner peace and dissolve as they regularly occur.

It is a bit like going to see a football match where you unconditionally support your team. But if they start to lose, you might surreptitiously change your shirt and move over to the other side. The idea is always to be on the winning side.

The winning side is always what actually happens. Nothing can beat that. If you expect something different, it does not automatically mean that reality changes. It means your expectations are invalid, out of date. It may be that, ultimately, the only thing you can trust is reality.

Your thoughts and expectations are based on how you have interpreted what you thought was happening over the years. All your expectations are by definition out of date, since things and even the very structure of things have changed since they were formed.

Can you internalize this very deeply? Buddhist tradition says that the last words of the Buddha to his monks were, "Everything changes. Do your best." Many people regard this as the quintessence of Buddhist thought.

Through study and meditation, as you begin to realize these things deeply, the gaps between your expectations or desires and reality, what is, cease to appear to you as problems and you experience more peace.

Ultimately you are unable to create a problem. You have stopped believing your thoughts. You work quietly to improve things but the gaps do not upset you. Life is easier.

Meditation

Write down what you expect to happen in the next minute, hour, day and week including when they will happen.

Find your historical learning and the cultural, parental and other influences that created these expectations.

Do you "know" what in fact will definitely happen?

If you do, what will you do if it does not happen?

If you do not, what is the meaning of your expectation?

Appreciate that your expectations are historical prejudices only and do not predict the present or the future.

10. IMPROVING YOUR DECISIONS AND AVOIDING GUILT

Understanding control and responsibility

"Buddhism never creates any guilt, it is not for repentance, it is for remembrance. The past is past; it is gone and gone forever—no need to worry about it. Just remember not to repeat the same mistakes again. Be more mindful."
- Osho[17]

How you make decisions

How can you enhance your decision making and responsibility and free yourself from guilt at the same time? People regularly ask me questions such as:

---

[17] Osho (Chandra Mohan Jain, 1931–1990): Indian mystic, guru and spiritual teacher.

"How can I decide if he is the right man for me? I want a family and time is running out."

"I have to choose one of these two jobs tomorrow but don't know how to decide."

"Should I have the operation? Two doctors recommend it strongly but my nutritionist says people have died from it and it doesn't always work anyway."

"I need money. Should I sell the Jeep or the Mercedes?"

How do you make correct decisions? What is a correct decision anyway?

Deciding things can be a tricky business. You may have realized in principle that your thoughts are empty, transparent and do not refer to anything real. But until you have thoroughly internalized this understanding, they continue to evoke emotions and actions, and they create and influence your life situations through your choices and decisions.

So how do you make good decisions? You may think the right decision is the one that produces the desired result, but unfortunately you have no result available at the time of your decision, so this does not help.

Another issue is guilt. When things do not work out you may have guilty feelings, characterized by thoughts that you should have decided differently.

You make decisions and choices all the time, many of which have serious effects on your life and other people's lives. In order to live with more peace of mind you need to comprehend the nature of decision-making. There are four things you need to understand:

The quality of your decision cannot be decided by the result.

You could not have acted differently.

When you decide between two or more alternatives, every alternative has apparent advantages and disadvantages.

Real things cannot be in conflict.

Let's examine these in more detail.

THE QUALITY OF YOUR DECISION CANNOT BE DECIDED BY THE RESULT

At the time of your decision there is no result. Many factors influence outcomes, including things you do not control and of which you are not even aware. A senior physician and head of a hospital department consulted me about his work stress due to having to decide correctly in life and death situations in his hospital. Here is the conversation:

Jack: I want to ask you something about my job. I find it very stressful
Jonathan: What is the stress?
Jack: I have to make decisions.
Jonathan: Of course, all the time, probably some serious ones, but where is the stress?
Jack: I can't make mistakes. People's health and even life depend on me.
Jonathan: I understand. It is a very responsible job. Do you in fact always decide right?
Jack: I have to.
Jonathan: I understand. But do you in fact? Always?

Jack: That is my job. I can't make mistakes. It is very stressful.
Jonathan: How long have you been practicing?
Jack: Over 40 years, including 12 as head of this department.
Jonathan: Did you ever make a mistake?
Jack: Yes. But I mustn't. That's the problem.
Jonathan: If you do in fact make mistakes, what do you mean by you mustn't make mistakes? What does that mean?
Jack: That is my job.
Jonathan: Is it possible to be a senior doctor with many years' experience without ever making a single mistake?
Jack: No.
Jonathan: How can it be your job to do something you know is impossible? What does that mean?
Jack: I see what you mean. *Relaxes slightly*
Jonathan: Do your decisions determine your patients' fate?
Jack: Sometimes, yes.
Jonathan: Is it possible for you to do everything right and still your patient dies?
Jack: Yes.
Jonathan: So how do your decisions determine your patients' fate?
Jack: Yes, I see. But don't I have influence?
Jonathan: Could you make a serious error but your patient might survive and recover. For example, if you prescribed the wrong drug late at night in an emergency, but the night nurse noticed your error and illegally corrected it, risking his neck to save the patient from your exhaustion?
Jack: I suppose so, yes.
Jonathan: So how do your decisions determine your patients' fate? Is it possible that other people and factors also contribute to the result?

Jack: Yes.
Jonathan: So what is the source of your stress? You seem to agree that you cannot in fact guarantee infallible decisions. You are, eventually, a human being with all its normal weaknesses. You also agreed there is no straight line from your decision to the patient's fate. There are other factors. So where exactly is the problem?
Jack: How to decide right. Each time, if I was sure, I could relax a bit. I get tense and worry.
Jonathan: Do you understand that there is absolutely no way to guarantee a right decision? Even with all your knowledge and experience, you will certainly make more mistakes. It is an occupational hazard. And that you alone do not determine what will happen?
Jack: Yes. But how can I worry less?
Jonathan: Firstly by realizing that, deep down.
Jack: Ok.
Jonathan: Then, knowing that you certainly will make mistakes, you do what you can to organize your shifts optimally, eat well, sleep well, include recreation and generally look after your own physical and mental health to the extent possible. It is not always easy in a hospital environment. You do what you can. You will feel better, and maybe even make a few less mistakes. That is the limit of your job. Is that acceptable?
Jack: Yes. That's ok. I can't do any more anyway.

YOU COULD NOT HAVE ACTED DIFFERENTLY

What you could have done is a thought. It has no existence beyond the thought. There is absolutely no way to determine what would have happened had you chosen differently. It is in fact meaningless, a fantasy, however much you believe it or however reasonable it seems. This is why you can never know the significance of a decision. There is no alternative in reality to what actually happens.

Guilt is your unrealistic expectation of perfection and the illusory belief that you could have acted differently. When you realize this, instead of being preoccupied with the past, you are more quietly connected to the present and tend to act more relevantly.

WHEN YOU DECIDE BETWEEN TWO OR MORE ALTERNATIVES, EVERY ALTERNATIVE HAS APPARENT ADVANTAGES AND DISADVANTAGES

Whichever way you go there are advantages and disadvantages. You lose and you gain each way. If there was a perfect alternative, if all the advantages were on one side and all the disadvantages on the other, there would have been no need to make a decision.

So in practice your job is to evaluate the usually unclear factors and see which alternative seems to have more overall benefit or less overall damage than the others. This process is always possible and involves no stress.

Remember that you always gain something and also lose something, possibly important things. You will also never know if you were right in any absolute sense, because you will never know what would have happened had you decided differently. That situation does not exist.

Also, there is no certain way of knowing the result in advance; since things change, no two situations are identical, so that there are no real precedents for action, only better or worse guesses.

REAL THINGS CANNOT BE IN CONFLICT

Your decisions occur every moment as part of your overall physical and mental being. When you feel you have to decide something, you may say you are in conflict. You may feel conflict between, for example, going to a football match and visiting your cousin in hospital for the third time this week.

Conflict is an emotional state. There are no conflicts in reality. If two real things were in conflict, one would not be there. Conflict is an idea, one particular way of interpreting a situation.

There are other ways of understanding this situation. For example, when a financial officer prepares a profit and loss statement, she writes down all the income and expenses. She does not regard the income and expenses as being in conflict. She calculates the bottom line, the profit or loss. It may be only one cent, but it is there—the result.

In all situations, you can only look for the bottom line—the way with more expected benefit or at least less harm. It is only your guess—in the real world things cannot be encapsulated neatly within concepts and logic. But it is your way.

The more you go your own way, guided by compassion and realism, the more the decisions you make are likely to be beneficial and less harmful. This builds your self-confidence, your trust in yourself and your peace of mind. That is the best you can do. Then nobody, including you, can reasonably complain.

This is a guilt-free way of living, and an easier way, with less stress. Each decision becomes an opportunity for your spiritual development.

Meditation

Sit quietly in a comfortable place.

Notice your breath going in and out for a few minutes.

Notice your thoughts as they come and go.

Consider a decision you will have to make soon.

List the options in your mind; list the pros and cons of each option.

Can you come to a conclusion regarding the overall benefit and harm of each option?

Is this conclusion an absolute fact or a hopefully well informed guess?

Notice the uncertainty in any choice you can make.

Can you behave in such a way as to ensure closure, that there will be no need for you to revisit the situation afterward, other than learning from experience?

11. Respecting Your Thoughts Without Believing Them

> Respect your thoughts, but as thoughts only; believing them is going too far

"We are what we think. All that we are arises with our thoughts. With our thoughts we make the world. Speak or act with a confused mind and trouble will follow you as the wheel follows the ox that draws the cart. Speak or act with a clear mind and happiness will follow you, as your shadow, unshakable."
- Buddha

Things Are Just What They Are

You do not see things. You can only see light, the light that enters your eyes. This light stimulates your optic nerves and sends messages to your brain. Your brain, or your mind, does not interpret what it sees; rather, it creates an original mental picture, albeit stimulated by what you see, but nevertheless a sublime work of art. You call this work of art by the name "reality" but in fact it is your creative genius working. The same applies to all your physical and mental senses.

It is a bit like the numbered dots that children join to make a picture. As Alan Watts[18] said, "Reality is only a Rorschach[19] ink-blot, you know."

Look at this:

Is it

    a collection of dots,

    a circle,

    or a square?

The dot collection, circle and square are all your mental creations. Cover the circle and square with your hand and look at the dots alone. Now imagine a circle or a square. The dots themselves remain what they are. This is how we create the world. When you appreciate this deeply, the imaginary world ceases to trouble you because it is not really there.

---

[18] Alan Watts (1915–1973): British philosopher, writer, speaker and interpreter of Eastern philosophy.
[19] The Rorschach inkblot test is a psychological test in which subjects' perceptions of inkblots are recorded and analyzed.

According to Buddhists your problems result from confusing a map for the territory it purports to represent and the menu for your meal. Maps and menus are very useful, as are thoughts, but have their limitations. You cannot smell the flowers on the map, eat the menu or think about reality. Ask yourself this question:

"What is this, if it is not what I think? What is it really?"

Ask yourself the same question regularly, in different life situations:

> when you are interested;
>
> when you are angry;
>
> when you are frightened;
>
> when you are depressed.

As you struggle with this question without finding an answer, since any answer is what you think, you will gradually come to realize you do not know. You do not know because, in reality, there is nothing to be known. All knowledge is thoughts. Reality is neither thoughts nor knowledge. It is.

As you realize this more and more deeply, stresses associated with anger, fear and depression disappear, since they are based on this confusion of identity. How can they possibly survive without the confusion? Ultimately your thoughts become transparent to you.

In the same way that others' opinions are of limited interest to you, so your own opinions cease to excite you. They remain practical tools like maps and menus, but nothing to get excited over. The excitement remains for reality.

This appreciation that your thoughts are empty, that they refer to nothing except themselves, is subtle, and the fact that you use your thoughts fairly successfully most of the time as maps, tempts you to believe in them. However, when the territory differs from the map, it is not the territory that is wrong but your map that is outdated or oversimplified.

The same goes for your thoughts. As you understand this more and more deeply, life gets easier.

Peter Fenner[20] once said the spiritual guide he would seek is someone who neither validates nor invalidates his structures. Validation and invalidation both imply that your thought or mental structures signify something real whereas actually they are just an expression of your amazing creativity. You can neither validate nor invalidate a work of art at a factual level, only aesthetically.

Keep asking yourself, "What is this, if not what I think? What is it really?"

Donovan's song "There is a mountain" popularized the Zen teaching of Qingyuan Weixin[21] which illustrates the appreciation of the territory beyond maps:

> "Before I had studied Zen for thirty years, I saw mountains as mountains, and rivers as rivers. When I arrived at a more intimate knowledge, I came to the point

---

[20] Peter Fenner (b. 1949): Australian philosopher, teacher and pioneer of the Western adaptation of nondual wisdom and psychotherapy.
[21] Qingyuan Weixin (960–1279) (Qing Yuan Weixin): Chinese monk who lived during the Song Dynasty.

where I saw that mountains are not mountains, and rivers are not rivers. But now that I have got its very substance I am at rest. For it's just that I see mountains again as mountains, and rivers once again as rivers."

– Adapted from Alan W. Watts: "The Way of Zen" Pantheon Books, Inc. 1957

Things are just what they are.

Meditation

Sit quietly in a comfortable place.

Notice your breath going in and out for a few minutes.

Look at your hand.

It is a hand.

Look at each finger in turn, starting with your thumb. Look at the skin. Feel the bones and sinews. Notice your nails.

Ask yourself: "Here are the fingers, here is the skin, here are the bones, here are the sinews, here are the nails… but where is the hand?

Try to grasp that what you call your hand is just a collection—of thumb, fingers, skin, bones, sinews and nails.

Can you take these away and leave your hand?

Can you take away your hand but leave your thumb, fingers, skin, bones, sinews and nails?

Try to grasp that "hand" is just the name of a collection. There is nothing tangible which is actually the hand.

Think of an art collection. Can you take away the pictures and leave the collection, or the opposite?

Look at your hand. It is there. But it is not a hand. You call it a hand but it itself is not a hand. "Hand" is an opinion about it, one among many ways of relating to it.

Try and grasp this deeply. It will free you from worrying about things which are not there. The world is what it is, but not the way you think about it.

As you begin to realize the truth of the situation, you will begin to feel the "hand" as a thought, floating between you and your physical hand.

First there is a hand;

Then there is a collection of thumb, fingers, skin, bones, sinews and nails;

Then there is… a hand.

Sometimes a hand is… well… just a hand.

Got it?

Meditate on this regularly. You can use your hand, your body, your mind, a car, a book or almost anything. As you internalize this realization, your life stresses lessen.

12. Cultivating Beneficial Relationships

Loving yourself and others unconditionally is a declaration of your sanity, since you are what you are anyway.

"We can live without religion but we cannot live without kindness."
- Dalai Lama

Underpinnings of stress-free relationships

Since you do not live totally alone in the world your relationships with other people are an integral part of your life. Trying to look after only yourself creates potential conflicts of interest in your mind between you and other people, with resulting mental tension. Family and other close relationships are typically the most loaded and complex but all relationships are potential sources of stress.

Understanding the nature of individuals and the relationships between them gives rise to a natural and simple conflict-free way of looking at and acting in interpersonal situations.

As your natural tendency to create benefit and avoid harm operates within a more and more realistic view of relationships, you find that instead of trying to balance your own needs against those of others, you feel and behave more in a way that tends to maximize overall benefit and minimize harm. As this space expands, less conflict and stress arise and life is easier.

There are three understandings involved in stress-free relationships that arise naturally from study and meditation:

> Awareness of the nature of individuals
>
> Awareness that discrimination has no real basis
>
> Unstructured listening or non-knowing

Awareness of the Nature of Individuals

Through study and meditation on the nature of reality and thoughts you become increasingly aware that your own thoughts do not actually refer to anything. You do not think about things. The mental picture of a flower in your mind is not the same thing as a real flower.

There is no need to look beyond a thought to find out what it refers to in the real world. Thoughts occur without referring to anything except themselves. Thoughts have no referent. In other words, your thoughts and opinions are transparent and empty of inherent significance.

The idea that you and other people are separate autonomous beings is an example of a thought. In reality you cannot find separate autonomous beings. For example, if you and I are in conversation, you have an effect on me. This affects the effect I have on you and so on. There is no beginning, no end and no controller of this interaction.

As you carefully examine your imagined perception of yourself as something separate and independent of the rest of the world you discover this perception to be empty. Your separate existence emerges more and more clearly as an idea rather than something real. You cannot find yourself as a real separate thing due to the multiple and largely unknown interdependencies between all phenomena including yourself. The same clearly applies to so-called others.

Awareness that Discrimination Has No Real Basis

Assuming that you prefer to be happy and not to suffer, the question is how to accomplish this efficiently. It is simply not possible to look after yourself alone, due to the multiple interconnections and interdependencies between us all.

Since you do not exist separately with real hermetically sealed boundaries you are inevitably affected by and affect other people and things, which in turn are affected by still more people and things.

Ultimately, you can see that the whole world cannot be realistically divided into separate phenomena. These exist only as thoughts, concepts or ideas.

As a result, the only effective way to look after yourself is to widen your area of interest to include the whole sphere of influence, everything together. By looking after everything with no discrimination or preference you effectively look after yourself as part of it. This involves less unpleasant and tiring conflicts which drain off your essential energy.

It is enough to generally improve things and avoid harm to the greatest extent possible. By looking beyond yourself to the happiness of all beings, the anxiety inherent in your imaginary central project of personal survival naturally dissolves. You look after yourself as a part of the whole thing, but with less conflict. This is the practical expression of compassion, love and kindness.

Albert Einstein[22] said:

> "A human being is part of the whole called by us universe, a part limited in time and space. We experience ourselves, our thoughts and feelings as something separate from the rest. A kind of optical delusion of consciousness. This delusion is a kind of prison for us, restricting us to our personal desires and to affection for a few persons nearest to us. Our task must be to free ourselves from the prison by widening our circle of compassion to embrace all living creatures and the whole of nature in its beauty. The true value of a human being is determined by the measure and the sense in which they have obtained liberation from the self. We shall require a substantially new manner of thinking if humanity is to survive."

---

[22] Albert Einstein (1879–1955): German-born theoretical physicist who developed the theory of general relativity. Einstein once said that he was not religious, but that had he been religious he would have been a Buddhist.

Although compassion, love and kindness are not the same they are closely related. Stephen Levine[23] said:

> "When your fear touches someone's pain it becomes pity. When your love touches someone's pain it becomes compassion."

I had the fortune to meet two great spiritual leaders, Rabbi Solomon David Sassoon[24] and the Dalai Lama. Both of them, when asked by journalists, "What is your religion?" answered, "Kindness."

Compassion is often misunderstood. Some people ask me whether they should be compassionate to themselves. Compassion is non-discriminatory love; there is no difference between being kind to yourself and others because there is in fact no real separation.

Buddha stated that you can search throughout the entire universe for someone who is more deserving of your love and affection than you are yourself, and that person is not to be found anywhere. You yourself, as much as anybody in the entire universe deserve your love and affection.

---

[23] Stephen Levine (b. 1937): American poet, author and teacher known for his work on death and dying through the teachings of Theravada Buddhism.
[24] Rabbi Solomon David Sassoon (1915–1985): British educator, rabbi, philanthropist, and collector of Jewish manuscripts.

Unstructured Listening or Non-Knowing

The main barrier to listening to someone is your knowledge of them. Your knowledge of people, as all knowledge, consists of your prejudices, the unconscious patterns of thinking you have accumulated.

If you know, there is no need to listen, the other person becomes redundant, a projection of your memories. These memories are evoked unconsciously. You find yourself responding not to the person in front of you, but to what they evoke, without your realizing this. You are then surprised when they get upset at your irrelevant reactions.

This way, you never really see or hear anyone and your responses are at best disconnected. People and situations become simply a mirror for your memories.

The trick is to become aware of the existence of the mirror, at which point at least you know you do not know, that there is nothing to be known. Then the potential for real listening may arise.

From this space of awareness you can begin to listen to another person without needing to know what they are saying, without categorizing their communication or having an opinion. Rather than adding your own personal historical significances you find yourself absorbing the communication as it is transmitted.

This is unstructured listening, the basis of all beneficial relationships and of effective psychotherapy.

Through this new way of listening you begin to realize that others' thoughts also, as expressed through their words, body language and other subliminal information, are similarly their habitual historical mental response to reality. You begin to appreciate that conversation between you consists of a dynamic interaction between two minds. This can be likened to a confluence of three rivers:

> Your historical tendencies;
>
> The other person's historical tendencies;
>
> Whatever is happening at the moment—the stream of reality, the natural order of things.

All three mutually influence each other. Neurological research indicates that during successful communication the speaker's and listener's brains exhibit joint, temporally coupled response patterns.

As you listen in a free, open way to the other person's thoughts, to your own thoughts and to everything else that is happening, you may become aware that some response is needed. Informed by compassion, non-discrimination and your resulting equal attitude to all, your actions follow naturally and quietly with neither intention nor effort.

Through meditation you sense the inner quiet that results from not trying. When you yourself listen and act from within this inner quiet you can better sense where people are and what is happening to them. Inner quiet is characterized by non-knowing.

Krishnamurti stated in his *Letters to the Schools* (Vol. I):

> The very nature of intelligence is sensitivity, and this sensitivity is love. Without this intelligence there can be no compassion. Compassion is not the doing of charitable acts or social reform; it is free from sentiment,

romanticism and emotional enthusiasm. It is as strong as death. It is like a great rock, immovable in the midst of confusion, misery and anxiety. Without this compassion no new culture or society can come into being. Compassion and intelligence walk together; they are not separate. Compassion acts through intelligence. It can never act through the intellect. Compassion is the essence of the wholeness of life.

MEDITATION

You are going to enjoy this!

Try arguing with someone about a controversial subject, as a game.

Try arguing a second time but without using your opinions.

Try arguing a third time, while both of you attempt to distinguish facts from opinions moment by moment.

Listen, as an outside observer or witness, to their and your own opinions expressing themselves freely in the dialog.

Notice that your opinions are both reflections of your personalities, formed by your histories, and cannot really be in conflict any more than two rivers. They flow as part of the overall dynamics of the interaction.

Enjoy your confusion.

That is all.

13. GENERATING IMMUNITY TO PRAISE AND CRITICISM

Becoming free from the opinions of others

"The wind cannot shake a mountain. Neither praise nor blame moves the wise man."
- Buddha

REALIZING WHO YOU REALLY ARE

It is easy to find out what you really are. You are not what you think. If you think you are not what you think, you are not that either.

You are also not what others think you are. If you eliminate everything you and others think about you, what is left is really you. Some people may think you are clever and others may think you are stupid. In both cases you are still what you are. That is all.

It is like standing in a hall of mirrors. Depending on which mirror you look in, you seem tall, short, fat, thin or distorted in other ways. But there is a real you which is none of these, standing there looking in the mirrors.

Your opinion about yourself is an expression of your mental history. Whether you feel strong or weak, optimistic or pessimistic, these are traces of the habitual ways you have internalized your life experiences, a process starting long before your birth, even before your mother's birth.

Research shows that a fetus, sharing its mother's bloodstream, reacts to its mother's hormonal changes and moods. Learning the nature of things started long ago.

Other people's opinions about you are similarly expressions of their mental history. Can you watch these histories expressing themselves? They do not tell you who you are but they do tell you something about the historical conditioning of whoever holds these opinions.

When you realize this, both your and others' opinions cease to disturb you. You watch them as you watch the waves on the beach.

In India there was a tradition of standing in the presence of a teacher out of respect. Two friends approached a group of students sitting with their teacher. One of them was shocked by this sight and asked his friend, "What is this? Why are they sitting?" His friend answered, "You say they are sitting only because you are standing."

All opinions exist only through their opposites. The *Tao Te Ching* states:

> "Under heaven all can see beauty as beauty only because there is ugliness.
>
> All can know good as good only because there is evil.

Therefore having and not having arise together.

Difficult and easy complement each other.

Long and short contrast each other;

High and low rest upon each other;

Voice and sound harmonize each other;

Front and back follow one another.

Therefore the sage goes about doing nothing, teaching no-talking.

The ten thousand things rise and fall without cease,

Creating, yet not possessing;

Working, yet not taking credit.

Work is done, then forgotten.

Therefore it lasts forever."

— Translated by Gia-Fu Feng and Jane English, 1972

When you clearly see the difference between opinions and reality, you are immune to both praise and criticism. Opinions are opinions. You are what you are.

MEDITATION

Write a one-page personal profile of yourself. Describe yourself and list your opinions about who and what you are.

Ask someone else to write a one-page profile of you. Ask them to describe you and list their opinions about you.

Compare them.

Write down who you really are, if not what you think and not what the other person thinks you are.

What are you if not that either?

Where does this end?

What are you really?

…?

14. ACHIEVING TOTAL FREEDOM

> Freedom is total when it includes freedom even from the need to be free

A young monk asked Master Shih-t'ou:[25] "How can I ever get emancipated?" The Master replied: "Who has ever put you in bondage?"

WHY FREEDOM CANNOT BE ACHIEVED

Freedom is an illusion. When you try to achieve freedom, that effort imprisons you. The effort to be free creates the idea that you are not free. This is your imaginary prison.

You will not understand this if you imagine I am referring to a physical prison with guards, dogs and barbed wire. Freedom is doing what you do. When you do something possible you

---

[25] Shih-t'ou: eighth century Chinese Chan (Zen) Buddhist teacher and author.

are free. When you try to do something impossible you are bound.

The only possible thing you can do is what you are doing, since you can never do anything except what you do. The feeling that you are bound stems from your thought that you should be doing something different from what you are actually doing, which is totally impossible.

As the Tibetans say:

> I think what I think.
>
> I do what I do.
>
> What happens, happens.

It is possible to be free inside a maximum security prison. Read about Nelson Mandela's experiences on Robben Island.[26]

Many people outside prisons feel imprisoned because they want to live differently, for example in a different job, with a different partner or in a different country.

Always remember:

> Things are never different from what they are.
>
> What happens, happens. Nothing else happens.
>
> *Trying* creates mental prisons. *Doing* does not.

---

[26] Nelson Mandela (1918–2013): South African anti-apartheid revolutionary, politician and philanthropist who served as President of South Africa from 1994 to 1999. 18 of his 27 prison years were spent on Robben Island.

If you can improve things, do it.

If you cannot, do not.

Never try, just act. Or not.

That is all.

Meditation

Are you free now?

If you are, what are you free of?

If you are not, what is binding you?

15. Fulfilling Yourself Now

> The aim of a Zen master is total fulfillment each moment, including the moment of death. There is no other aim.

"The sage stays behind, thus he is ahead. He is detached, thus at one with all. Through selfless action, he attains fulfillment."
- Lao Tzu (trans. Gia-Fu Feng and Jane English, 1972)

Being as You Are

The Buddha did not try to be someone else. He was consciously himself. If you are consciously yourself you are Buddha. Rabbi Zusha[27] said that in Heaven he would not be asked why he was not like the prophet Moses but rather why he was not like Rabbi Zusha.

---

[27] Rabbi Zusha (1718–1800): Meshulam Zusha of Anipoli, renowned Chasidic master born in Galicia, Southeast Poland.

You tend to identify fulfillment with achieving or being something. Some elderly people say they refuse to die until their grandchildren are married. However, since you do not control the future, this creates anxiety as your prize is uncertain. The other way is that of a Zen master whose sole aim is to fulfill him/herself totally each moment.

Each moment you respond appropriately and with total responsibility, you are by definition totally fulfilled, since there is nothing else to do. But how can you know what is appropriate and how to be totally responsible? You cannot judge your behavior by the results since you do not know what would have happened otherwise. History has only one line leading always to where we are now. Does that mean you have no responsibility?

Responsibility can be regarded as your ability to respond appropriately to each situation you encounter, moment by moment. In order to respond appropriately you need two things:

To see things as they are;

Positive intention.

In order to see things as they are it is necessary to distinguish between what is and what you think is. This means knowing what is real and what is not.

Everything is real except for what you think. The more you distinguish reality from what you think, the less likely you are to behave in accordance with your historical conditioning and the more likely to respond relevantly to what is actually happening. Otherwise, even with the best of intentions, you may be creating damage.

You already have a positive intention to be happy and to avoid suffering. This seems to be a universal characteristic. As you realize more and more the inseparability of things, the interdependence of phenomena, this positive intention naturally widens, ultimately including everyone and everything.

Acting and thinking without involvement, from your unconditioned mind, free of prejudices, you do what needs to be done now and life is a lot easier

One of the indicators of your progress in meditation is that things get done with less and less mental effort, and ultimately with none at all. You find yourself experiencing meditation and life in general, rather than trying to get everything into shape. Your actions are spontaneous. Fulfillment occurs naturally each aware moment without conscious effort. It is totally independent of the future, which is no more than a fantasy anyway.

Meditation

Are you responding right now to what is happening or to what you think is happening?

Are you trying to do something or just doing it?

Check if you are behaving relevantly now.

What is relevant if not what you think?

16. EFFORTLESS SURVIVAL

When you realize that you are not what you think you are, you no longer have to worry about surviving. You cannot die since you were never born. This realization brings great peace.

"As long as the 'me' survives in any form, very subtly or grossly, there must be violence."
- Krishnamurti

THERE IS NOTHING TO SURVIVE

Your thoughts create an idea of "I," who you believe you are. Psychologists call this your self-image. One way of discovering your self-image is to ask yourself the question, "Who am I?" Any answer you give is by necessity a thought, your opinion about yourself, not who you really are. Who are you really then, if not what you think?

There are two central errors in meditation. One is to believe you exist and the other is to believe you do not exist. In both cases you believe there is something real called "I" that may exist or not exist.

When you realize that neither of these applies, that "I" is an idea, you are no longer worried about your survival and life is easier. You do what you do and things happen.

If you watch the sea, although the waves seem to exist, they are not different from the water, and the water is not different from the sea. The waves are temporary forms of the water of the sea. The waves are neither created nor destroyed but appear to exist briefly as temporary configurations of the water.

Similarly your body and mental activity are changing forms of material and energy. Where was this material and energy a million years ago? Where will it be in a million years' time? The material and energy themselves are neither created nor destroyed.

What you call "I" is a temporary accumulation of material and energy, continually changing from long before your birth to long after your death.

When you say that a tree grows or that rain falls, you refer to natural processes. You do not look for who is growing the tree or moving the rain down. These processes occur as part of the way things are.

However, when you say you decide to write a letter, you do not believe you are referring only to a mental and physical process in which a decision appears and a hand moves a pen, in the same way that a tree grows or rain falls. There is also an implicit belief that *you* are deciding and acting, that *you* exist as an independent active agency.

Ask yourself what this "I" is, to which you refer. Is there something real and separate from your mind and body which controls them? Or are your mind and body also natural processes that happen without needing to invent someone who is controlling them? Maybe you are more like a tree than you realize.

This does not mean you cannot use the words "I" and "mine." They are convenient designations. Provided you remember that they do not refer to anything real, they do not cause you trouble.

Krishnamurti said, "As long as there is a meditator, there is no meditation."

Study and meditation may be essential to discover the truth of things and internalize the insights you learn. But as long as you believe *you* meditate, your meditation creates and reinforces your idea that you yourself exist, as something beyond a thought, which is doing the meditation.

Through special insight meditation, as you observe both your thoughts and the observer simultaneously, it becomes apparent that they are not different, that the idea of an observer at all is another of the thoughts. This understanding brings great relief.

Meditation

Observe your surroundings: listen to the sounds and watch everything around you.

Observe your body: notice your sensations including your breath going in and out.

Observe your mind: watch your thoughts and emotions.

Observe the observer: who is observing?

Find out who is observing the observer.

Where are you in this picture?

Ask yourself, "Who am I if not what I think I am?" Try to discover who you really are as a fact, independent of knowledge, thoughts and opinions, which cannot be disputed.

Try to establish the absolute truth of these things.

17. EXPLOITING EVERYTHING

What do you do when you have no idea what to do?

When written in Chinese, the word crisis is composed of two characters—one represents danger and the other represents opportunity
- John F. Kennedy[28]

MENTAL IMMUNITY

Your whole education was almost certainly centered round getting what you want, or at least what your parents wanted for you in life—a partner, career, health, money, social status and material, physical and mental satisfaction. This is fine as far as it goes.

What your education probably did not adequately include was the clear understanding that these things are not under your

---

[28] John F. Kennedy (1917–1963): the 35th President of the United States, from January 1961 until he was assassinated in November 1963.

sole control. Even if your parents told you to do your best and that that would be enough, in most cases they did not mean it. At best, in their hearts, they were trying to console themselves in advance for your failures to satisfy them. This may sound harsh, but as parents you also dearly want the best for your children. It is not an issue on which we easily compromise.

One of your fundamental misunderstandings is that you should close the gap between what is and what you want, that gaps mean something is wrong. Certainly your efforts will be in this direction.

When you are hungry you will naturally look for food. If you are looking for a restaurant you may pass ten shoe shops without noticing them but you will stop at the first restaurant and check it out. Conversely, if you want new shoes you may not notice the restaurants.

You can look for a restaurant happily or unhappily. I am not talking about your actions but about how you feel while you are acting. Looking for a restaurant does not in itself make you stressed, but getting annoyed that you have not found one yet, or that you did not go down a different street, makes you stressed.

You cannot solve all your problems in life. You cannot close all the gaps. Your peace of mind is threatened and destroyed only by believing that you can. Then, in addition to being hungry (in the above example), you are angry with yourself.

Through study, meditation and contact with a teacher, you realize that you do not even control your mind. Your mind operates as it does, a natural process far beyond your understanding, never mind control. You do not control your body. You certainly do not control your environment, the world and other people.

As you get used to the gaps, to the ups and downs in life as the nature of things, it all upsets you less. Your happiness and peace of mind become more independent of what is happening. You continue to work to close the gaps but their existence does not constitute a threat to your mental health.

You can even use the gaps between what you want and what is happening moment by moment as opportunities for your personal spiritual development.

Most gaps are small irritations:

> Someone takes your parking space.
>
> Your remote control battery finishes.
>
> You cannot find your keys.
>
> The cake does not rise.
>
> Your son does not want to get up for school.
>
> You have a headache.
>
> Your rival gets promotion.
>
> ...

Sometimes there are big gaps you call crises:

> Your partner leaves or dies.
>
> Your daughter gets involved in drugs.
>
> You get seriously ill.
>
> You lose your job.

Although crises are more difficult to negotiate, the small gaps are so frequent that you can use them as fuel for your own development by noticing both the situation and your mental construct of "it should not happen," which enables mental stress to arise. When you do this, instead of problems in life there are only opportunities.

As you practice this skill of awareness, the whole of life fuels it. Your mental immunity threshold gradually rises, converting more serious crises into yet more fuel. The process naturally snowballs.

Meditation

Get a notebook and write down every upsetting thing that happens. Nothing is too trivial or too big. For each event, note:

> *The date and time;*
>
> *What actually happened (reality);*
>
> *What should have happened (a thought).*

Become aware of the fundamental difference between reality and what you think. Only your thought structure enables your stress.

If you find yourself critical of your reactions, restart the process but this time examine your reaction itself by noting:

> *Your actual reaction (reality);*
>
> *How you should have reacted (a thought);*
>
> *Continue this until you understand.*

18. DISCOVERING THAT THERE IS NOTHING SPECIAL TO DO

Do whatever you are doing. There is nothing else you can ever do.

"I think what I think. I do what I do. What happens, happens."
- Tibetan Kagyu[29] saying

REALITY IS NEVER DIFFERENT FROM WHAT IS

The Buddha stated that release from mental stress occurs as a result of grasping the true nature of things. In one of the dialogues of Joshu:[30]

---

[29] Kagyu: one of the four main schools of Tibetan Buddhism, together with the Nyingma, Sakya and Gelug.
[30] Joshu (Chinese Zhàozhōu, 778–897): Chan (Zen) Buddhist master known for his paradoxical statements and unusual actions.

> A monk asked, When I wish to become a Buddha, what then?
>
> Joshu said, "You have set yourself quite a task, haven't you?"
>
> The monk said, "When there is no effort—what then?"
>
> Joshu said, "Then you are a Buddha already."

In a dialogue between Joshu and his master Nansen

> Joshu asked [his master] Nansen, "The Way—what is it?"
>
> Nansen said, "It is everyday mind."
>
> Joshu said, "One should then aim at this, shouldn't one?"
>
> Nansen said, "The moment you aim at anything, you have already missed it."
>
> Joshu said, "If I do not aim at it, how can I know the Way?"
>
> Nansen said, "The Way has nothing to do with knowing or not knowing." Knowing is perceiving but blindly. Not knowing is just blankness. If you have already reached the un-aimed-at Way, it is like space: absolutely clear void. You cannot force it one way or the other."
>
> *At that instant* Joshu was awakened to the profound meaning. His mind was like the bright full moon.
>
> – Quoted in Joshu, 1978.

Longchen Rabjam described the result:

> "Like an easygoing person who has completed his work—body and mind rest in any way that is comfortable."

He explained further:

> "Liberation is achieved by correctly grasping the nature of mind, the nature of all phenomena. Then there is no further peace to be attained."

When you grasp your true nature and the identical nature of the world, you find yourself in the unconditioned mind, where not only is there no conflict, but it is clear that even the possibility of conflict does not exist. The mechanism for creating conflict is absent. Physical and mental pain may occur, but are not interpreted as problems and so remain sensations only. The world, including you, does whatever it does. There is no disturbance and no-one who could possibly be disturbed.

In this clear mental space there is just what there is. All that remains is infinite love, unbounded compassion. Boundaries are recognized neither as present nor absent. Compassion is undiscriminating because no separate things are recognized between which discrimination can occur. Your natural desire to be happy and to avoid suffering identifies effortlessly with all beings.

The illusory dream world structured by your mind continues to play according to your conditioning but since you are aware of it as a dream it neither confuses nor confounds you. No harm occurs since there is nothing to cause harm, nothing to be harmed and no mechanism by which harm can occur.

Gradually the dream itself fades and a deep serenity infuses all being. Spontaneous activity replaces effort. It is said that the master, by doing nothing, achieves all. This does not mean you do nothing but rather that the doing happens without the need for *you* to do it, just as day and night occur spontaneously.

In this nondual mental space the two basic elements of full awakening arise spontaneously, co-emergent and coalescent, distinct and unseparated:

> **Wisdom**—seeing things as they are, the recognition of all possible thoughts and mental structures as empty space;
>
> **Compassion**—absence of discrimination expressed through equal deep respect for your own and others' thoughts and mental structures, which create your and their apparent worlds.

Avalokiteshvara,[31] the Bodhisattva[32] of Compassion, clarified to Sariputra[33] in the Prajnaparamita:[34]

> *There is neither ignorance nor an end to ignorance;*
>
> *There is neither old age and death nor an end to old age and death;*
>
> *There is no suffering, no cause of suffering, no end to suffering and no path to follow;*
>
> *There is no attainment of wisdom and no wisdom to attain.*

There is neither a need to let go of, nor retain anything.

---

[31] Avalokiteshvara: a bodhisattva (see next note) who embodies the compassion of all Buddhas, widely revered in Mahayana Buddhism.
[32] Bodhisattva: in Buddhist tradition, the embodiment of bodhicitta, the spontaneous wish to attain Buddhahood for the benefit of all sentient beings.
[33] Sariputra: one of two chief male disciples of the Buddha.
[34] Prajnaparamita: "The Perfection of Wisdom," a central understanding in Mahayana Buddhism, regarded as an essential element of the Bodhisattva Path. The practice of Prajnaparamita is detailed in texts ranging from 1 to 100,000 verses, all of which are regarded as having identical essential content, namely that all things, including itself, appear as conceptual constructs.

By learning we discover that there was never anything to be learnt.

Through meditation we appreciate that meditation is unnecessary.

True understanding is the understanding that there is nothing real to be understood.

The ultimate achievement is knowing that there is nothing to achieve.

The only thing you need to do is what you are already doing. Since you are already doing that and no other possibility exists, no specific mental effort or physical action is required to achieve it.

MEDITATION

Live your life fully

PART 2. REALIZING

19. ABOUT MEDITATION

Getting used to being fully awake

"Meditation brings wisdom; lack of meditation leaves ignorance. Know well what leads you forward and what holds you back, and choose the path that leads to wisdom."
- Buddha

CONNECTING TO REALITY

Meditation is being awake.

Meditation is being awake.

Being awake is awareness.

Awareness is presence.

Presence is listening.

Listening is being fully connected to reality, what is actually happening, now.

Sit in a pleasant, comfortable place.

Listen to the sounds.

Far-off sounds, near sounds.

Important sounds, insignificant sounds.

The sounds change every moment.

Your memory and thoughts are of no help in knowing what sounds there are now.

Only listening, attention can tell you what sounds there are now.

Notice the sounds. You hear them, then they are gone.

Everything is temporary. Everything changes. Everything passes.

All you really have is the experience of this moment.

As you listen, the experience becomes only a memory.

But a new experience appears.

Enjoy the experience.

You are alive.

That is all.

ABOUT MEDITATION

Meditation comprises a family of techniques to help connect you better to reality until you realize reality as your nature. There is no need to isolate yourself in a monastery, cave or remote forest or leave your job or family, although some people find these options conducive to meditation. There is no right or wrong way to sit; in fact you may not be sitting at all. It is enough to spend some quiet time with yourself every day. This may turn out to be your most precious gift, from you to yourself, given with unconditional love.

Opportunities present themselves. You may be sitting at a red traffic light or waiting for a friend or a client and have nothing special that needs to be done at that moment. This is an opportunity for meditation, for getting used to noticing your surroundings, your body and your thoughts and emotions as they change from moment to moment.

As you continue to meditate, you become aware of more and more opportunities, until eventually you find yourself naturally in a meditative state all the time, even while your normal activities continue as usual. You reach the point at which, as Dudjom Rinpoche,[35] one of Tibet's foremost yogis, scholars, and meditation masters said, "Even though the meditator may leave the meditation, the meditation does not leave the meditator."

Obstacles

The main obstacle to meditation is thinking that you need to do or to avoid doing something particular, or indeed that you are meditating. Krishnamurti said, "Any form of conscious meditation is no meditation."

Essentially, it is impossible to meditate incorrectly. More precisely, the only way to meditate incorrectly is to try to meditate correctly. What happens, happens. This poem illustrates the point:

> *Nothing whatever that you can do can change what is happening now*

---

[35] Dudjom Rinpoche (1904–1987): Tibetan yogi, writer and Dzogchen master, teacher of the 14th Dalai Lama's Dzogchen teachers, Dilgo Khyentse Rinpoche and Trulshik Rinpoche.

Simply because whatever you are doing is not different from what is happening

No one in particular is doing it

The river flows naturally

Enjoy it

Take it easy

Or not

Either way

20. FAMILIES OF BUDDHIST MEDITATION

There are two ways to improve your differentiation between thoughts and absolute reality, the truth, which can be used separately or combined. In Buddhist terminology these are:

Shamatha: tranquility meditation

Vipashyana: special insight meditation

SHAMATHA: TRANQUILITY MEDITATION

Tranquility meditation involves paying close attention to what you actually experience each moment, using your physical and mental senses to notice the occurrence of your thoughts, emotions and sensations as part of this experience.

Tranquility meditation is used to reduce anxiety, cultivate concentration and generate a relatively quiet state where thoughts cannot disturb you. It enhances your seeing, hearing and other senses, and enables you to read others' minds more clearly so that you can better serve their needs and cultivate compassion, the cornerstone of your personal development.

Imagine yourself walking in a sand storm able to see only ten centimeters forward. Gradually, the wind calms and you begin to see and hear things you missed before. You see a tree; you hear a squirrel moving in the grass.

Normally, your thoughts—the grains of your personal sand storm—prevent you from seeing yourself, other people, objects and situations as they really are. As you learn to recognize your thoughts as thoughts only, the confusion calms and ultimately disappears, leaving you with things as they really are. Thoughts will always be a part of you but you can learn to cease relating to them as if they represent something real.

Vipashyana—Special Insight Meditation

Using insight meditation, you observe, analyze and deconstruct non-reality, what you think, until it naturally dissolves. You rigorously investigate your mental constructs and processes including your thoughts, beliefs, judgments, memories and expectations, to establish clearly for yourself that all apparently perceived or identified external phenomena, thoughts, the mind and "I" are mental structures that do not refer to anything real.

> **Insight meditation** is used to observe the mind.
>
> **Special insight meditation** is used to investigate and discover the nature of your mind. Using special insight meditation, you examine the nature of thoughts, the resting mind, the observer, awareness and experience itself.

Non-Meditation

As you become more familiar with tranquility and insight meditation, you may begin to find yourself resting in non-meditation. Non-meditation is meditation in the sense that there is awareness but not in the sense that someone is meditating.

Ultimately, meditation shows you that there is no one meditating and no meditation to be practiced. As you study and meditate, preferably with the guidance of a teacher, you achieve:

> The appreciation that all identified phenomena are in fact thoughts.
>
> The recognition that thoughts are also identified phenomena, and therefore ungraspable.
>
> The understanding that there is neither an observer nor absence of an observer.
>
> The ability to focus on nothing, which is everything, cultivating spaciousness.
>
> The realization that there is in fact nothing special for you to do.

The following sections explain this process in more detail, to provide practical methods for achieving unconditional peace of mind and happiness.

21. STAGES OF MEDITATION

There are many well-defined paths of meditation employed by different Buddhist traditions. If you want, you can study some of them in detail.

Here is one simplified approach in a preparation stage followed by seven meditation stages. Initially you can spend, say, ten minutes on each stage. However, each stage may require up to two years to achieve the corresponding state of realization, before progressing to the next stage.

In practice, following the first two stages, you may find yourself naturally beginning to practice the stages together. The effectiveness of the later stages depends on what level you have achieved in the earlier stages. At any point you can use whichever level you feel most contributes to your understanding and peace of mind in the context in which you find yourself.

These instructions are not intended to replace a teacher. Your teacher provides the inspiration, love, and life-blood that bring the exercises to life. Used alone, the exercises are dry, with limited impact, but with a teacher they can be used as valuable reminders, since we regularly forget.

Stages one and two are inspired by Buddhist tranquility meditation. Stages three through seven are inspired by Tibetan Mahamudra special insight practices in a partial, simplified and condensed form. The bibliography on my website[36] includes references to more advanced manuals on these methods.

Here are the stages:

> **Preparation stage**
>
> **Stage one**: Observing your environment
>
> **Stage two**: Observing your sensations
>
> **Stage three**: Observing your mind
>
> **Stage four**: Observing the observer
>
> **Stage five**: Accessing the awareness that is aware of itself
>
> **Stage six**: Resting in non-meditation
>
> **Stage seven**: Nothing special

PREPARATION

Sit comfortably with your back straight. If you sit on a cushion your bottom should be higher than your knees so that your back straightens naturally. If you sit on a chair, adjust your feet so that your knees are naturally in line with your feet such that minimum effort is required to maintain

---

[36] Bibliography on my website: https://endingstress.org/reading-suggestions/

your posture. This way you are not preoccupied with your body so are free to concentrate on the meditation. Lying down is not recommended for beginners, due the natural tendency to fall asleep.

Leave your eyes naturally open. The idea of meditation is to connect to reality, not to disconnect, and seeing is a primary human sense.

If you like to practice yoga or relaxation, do these before meditating. Meditation should be the last stage.

STAGE ONE: OBSERVING YOUR ENVIRONMENT

Listening

Listen to the sounds in the room.

Listen to the sounds outside the room.

Listen to the sounds in your body. If you are quiet you can hear your heartbeat.

Listen to the sounds you can identify and the sounds you cannot identify.

Notice that the sounds are different each moment. No two moments are identical. Everything changes.

Notice that you do not control the sounds. You listen while the sounds happen.

Whenever you notice you have forgotten the listening and are occupied in thinking, notice the thought and return to the sounds. Each such moment increases awareness of the existence of the thought and discriminates it from the more tangible experience of listening.

Watching

Choose a spot on the floor so you look down at about 45 degrees or a spot on the opposite wall at eye level. Do not use something that moves, such as a candle flame. Do not use anything that evokes strong emotions such as family pictures. Natural things such as a leaf or flower are good.

Gently watch your chosen spot. Whenever you notice you have forgotten the watching and are occupied in thinking, notice the thought and return to the watching. Each such moment increases awareness of the existence of the thought and discriminates it from the experience of watching.

Listen and watch simultaneously. Whenever you notice you have forgotten the listening and watching and are occupied in thinking, notice the thought and return to the listening and watching. Each such moment increases awareness of the existence of the thought and discriminates it from the experience of listening and watching.

STAGE TWO: OBSERVING YOUR SENSATIONS

Notice the sensations in the different parts of your body.

Whenever you notice you have forgotten your bodily sensations and are occupied in thinking, notice the thought and return to sensing your body.

Each such moment increases awareness of the existence of the thought and discriminates it from the experience of your sensations in:

Your toes;

Your feet;

your ankles;

your legs;

your knees;

your thighs;

your stomach and internal organs;

your chest in the region of your heart;

your throat;

your chin, jaws, cheeks and ears;

your lips;

your nose and the surrounding area;

your eyes, temples and the space between your eyes;

your head;

the back of your neck;

your upper arms;

your elbows;

your lower arms;

your wrists;

your hands to the tips of your fingers, the space between your fingers and your palms;

your shoulders;

your upper back;

your middle back;

your lower back;

your bottom;

your thighs from behind;

your knees from behind;

your calves;

your heels;

the soles of your feet.

Rest for a few minutes while focusing on your bodily sensations.

Now transfer your attention to your breathing.

Watch your breath go in and out.

There is no special way to breathe. Just watch how your body wants to breathe naturally.

Notice that each breath is different. No two breaths are identical.

Whenever you notice you have forgotten your breathing and are occupied in thinking, notice the thought and return to watching your breathing. Each such moment increases awareness of the existence of the thought and discriminates it from the experience of breathing.

STAGE THREE: OBSERVING YOUR MIND

In this stage you begin to examine the nature of mind. In the previous exercises you observed your surroundings, your body and your breathing. Whenever you noticed you had stopped observing and were occupied in thinking, you noticed the thought and returned to observing your surroundings, your body and your breathing.

These exercises create an initial ability to begin to observe thoughts themselves. In this exercise you will deepen that ability.

Start by watching your breathing. Each time you notice a thought, return your attention to your breathing.

Get used to this for a few minutes, allowing yourself to discriminate between the physical sensation of breathing and the mental sensation of thinking. Note that:

> Your breathing is really happening;
>
> Your thoughts really occur;
>
> What you think, the stories, are not part of what is happening; they reflect your creativity and mental history.

When you feel yourself returning regularly from your thoughts to your breathing over and over again, begin to very gently transfer the focus of your attention to the thoughts themselves:

> Watch your thoughts.
>
> Notice how they arise, stay a few moments and dissolve.
>
> Notice your many kinds of thoughts including memories, expectations, opinions, beliefs and others.

Here are some useful metaphors for watching your thoughts. If none of them suit you, feel free to invent your own metaphor:

> See your thoughts float past you on a screen like a movie.

Watch each thought as a scrap of printed paper blowing in the wind.

See each thought as a labeled, colored balloon blowing in the wind; watch the balloons rising in front of you and floating off into the sky; watch them as they get smaller and eventually disappear from view.

Now, begin to examine each thought in detail. Try to arrive at clear conclusions regarding the following key questions. Your conclusion may be that it is impossible to reach clear conclusions. If so, find out why.

As the thought appears: What is the physical source of the thought? Where does the thought come from? What happens at the moment of birth of the thought? Where are all the future thoughts you have not yet thought?

While the thought exists: Look into the thought—what is its nature? What are its characteristics? Does the thought have a height, width or depth? Does it have a color? Does it have an inside and outside or not? Can you reach definitive conclusions as inarguable facts, or are all these questions inappropriate to thoughts?

As the thought disappears: Where does the thought go? What exactly happens at the moment of disappearance? Where are all the thoughts you have thought in the past?

Between the thoughts: When a thought disappears there is sometimes a gap of a few moments before the next thought arises. Look into this gap. What do you see there? What is the nature of this settled mind in contrast to the mind in motion with thoughts? Is the settled mind the same as the mind in motion, but with the addition of thoughts? Are the thoughts and the settled mind the same—just as the sea, the water and the waves are the same—or different?

You may reach conclusions, you may not. Concluding that there is no conclusion is in itself a conclusion. No one can tell you, as it is your experience.

You may experience confusion or even anxiety. If these are tolerable, persist in the analysis of the nature of mind. If they become intolerable, gently return to focus on your breathing. As you calm down, you may feel like returning to examining the nature of your mind.

You can move between tranquility and special insight meditations freely. You can neither succeed nor fail in the analysis of mind. The consistent examination and attempt to reach conclusions clarifies and deepens your awareness. That is the object of the exercise.

STAGE FOUR: OBSERVING THE OBSERVER

Repeat stage three. Get used to sitting quietly observing your mind and thoughts. The experience of your mind and thoughts is undeniable. You can sense it happening.

When you have a reasonably clear and stable perception of your mind thinking, turn your attention to the observer. Establish who or what is actually observing your mind. If the answer is "I, find out what that means:

What is the observer?

Where is the observer?

Is the observer separate from the experience?

If so, where and what are these two things? What is the difference between them?

If you conclude that the observer is not different from the experience, why do you use two words?

Try to reach definitive inarguable conclusions.

STAGE FIVE: ACCESSING THE AWARENESS THAT IS AWARE OF ITSELF

As you repeat stages one through four over weeks, months and years, the distinctions between your experience, thoughts, mind and yourself as the observer blur. It becomes increasingly clear that these distinctions, and even the separate existence of your experience and the observer are only more ideas, more thoughts.

You become gradually aware that the only thing to which you can point with reasonable confidence is your experience itself.

You naturally begin to relax and the experience happens. Your mental events begin to arise for you in a space of pure awareness.

Ultimately there is no distinction for you between experience, thoughts, mind, observer and awareness. You become naturally aware of awareness itself, and this awareness is not different from the experience. At this point it is unclear whether or not you yourself are present, and it becomes unimportant.

Stage six: Resting in non-meditation

As the experience itself gains center stage, leaving behind the actors including yourself, you find yourself resting in non-meditation. The meditation is there in the form of the experience but there is no meditator.

Stage seven: Nothing special

It is clear that what happens, happens. There is and never was anything else. Characteristic of this last stage is the clear realization that there were never any stages. There was never meditation. There was neither a meditator nor even the absence of a meditator. Longchen Rabjam stated in *The Precious Treasury of the Way of Abiding* (Longchen Rabjam 1998):

> "There is simply the illusion of difference based on whether or not awareness is recognized."

And in his commentary he clarified:

> "However the mind stirs, if this is understood to be the display of naturally occurring timeless awareness (like waves on water), just by letting go, freedom comes about in the nonduality of mental states of abiding and stirring."

In fact there is not even a need for letting go, merely the awareness that there was never anything you need to let go, no one to let go, and that letting go itself is merely another thought, part of the overall experience.

There is ultimately nothing special to do.

Live your life fully.

Frequently Asked Questions

Answers are often obvious. The difficulty may be in asking the right question. It is not a case of "thinking out of the box" but rather the realization that there never was a box anyway

"To raise new questions, new possibilities, to regard old problems from a new angle, requires creative imagination and marks real advance in science."
- *Albert Einstein*

What does "nondual" mean?

Dualistic thinking occurs in concepts, pairs of complementary categories such as "I" and "the world" or "good" and "bad," which appear to split everything into two parts, hence *duality*. This type of thinking enables conflict and mental tension to occur. Examples include the feeling that "I" must get what I need from "the world," or war where each side believes it is the "good" opposing the "bad."

Splitting, judgment and mental tension require two things, in order that these can be compared. However, the real world is neither inherently split nor unified. All splitting or unification is arbitrary. These are your mental processes, your attitude to things, not things themselves as they really are.

As you begin to realize that two and one are both thoughts, that the real world is neither inherently split nor whole, neither two nor one but just what it is, conflict and mental tension collapse and disappear. This is nondual meditation.

You cannot compare reality with anything else in order to decide whether it is correct or not, as there is nothing else.

You may need to study and practice various dualistic meditations with well-defined aims as a mental preparation for nondual meditation.

Doesn't all this lead to apathy?

Do you want to be happy and to not suffer? If this is not the case, if you are indifferent or apathetic regarding yourself, this may be an expression of depression, a psychological or psychiatric condition. There are experts in such matters.

However, if you are concerned with your own happiness and absence of suffering, then the realization that we are all connected, that we depend on each other mutually in many ways we do not begin to understand, leads naturally to widening your area of interest to include everything and everyone.

Realizing that we are all similar with common basic needs leads to a broader concern. Then two questions naturally arise each moment: "What is happening now?" and "Can I improve things?" Of course, what constitutes improvement is often unclear and in any case dependent on circumstances. However, even the presence of this motivation increases the chance of a useful outcome.

This desire is not directed at any particular person but at everyone including yourself. This is responsibility, unconditional love or compassion, possibly the opposite of apathy.

CANNOT ANGER BE A POSITIVE FORCE FOR CHANGE?

We use the word anger in two ways:

To be angry with someone: sometimes you need to use force including shouting or even physical force to prevent or restrain undesirable behavior. This does not necessarily cause trouble. It all depends on your motivation and the circumstances.

To experience anger inside: when we experience anger, there are mental and physical dimensions. We feel stress, we may sweat, have violent thoughts of revenge. This is both unpleasant and has the potential for damage to ourselves and others. We are not completely sane, our judgment is distorted and we tend to think in extremes. Our behavior is likely to be inappropriate.

Although a situation sometimes calls for the use of verbal or physical force, if we behave from a place of sanity, quietly, with the deep intention to reduce suffering and increase happiness, it is less likely that trouble will result.

The central factor is your intention.

Nevertheless, sometimes we do get angry. The main thing then is not to be angry that we are angry. This quickly spirals out of control. If you are angry, then just be angry. That is what is happening at that moment. This way the energy of the anger dissipates faster.

Mahatma Gandhi[37] said, "It is better not to be angry. But if you are angry, it is better to express it."

IF THERE IS NO "I," WHO MEDITATES?

There are two central errors of understanding: the belief that you exist and the belief that you do not exist. Both depend on a more fundamental error: that the word or concept or thought "I" signifies something real. When you look for this thing and find nothing, both of these beliefs dissolve, leaving pure awareness. At this point, the question does not arise at all. There is meditation without the need for a meditator, just as there is rain without a "rainer" and wind without a blower.

WHAT IS THE CONNECTION BETWEEN MEDITATION AND MORALITY?

Morality is the active expression of unconditional love, compassion, the equalizing of attitude to yourself and others with the desire for benefit and avoiding harm to the greatest extent possible. In order to achieve this you need an accurate appraisal of what is happening, otherwise, even with your best intentions, your actions may cause unintended harm.

---

[37] Mahatma Gandhi (Mohandas Karamchand Gandhi, 1869–1948): the leader of Indian nationalism in British-ruled India. Widely known for his encouragement to practice non-violence and truth in all situations.

What is happening is not the same as what you think is happening. What you and other people are is not what you think they are. Believing that you are separate has no real basis beyond your mental activity.

What you think is largely determined or at least influenced by your mental biography, the unconscious patterns and understandings of yourself and the world acquired over years of interpreting experiences. If you believe what you think, you live in a historical dream. In order to know what is really happening, you need to get used to being awake. That is meditation, the foundation of morality.

I MEDITATE AND STUDY BUT CANNOT CONNECT THEM. HOW IS MEDITATION SUPPOSED TO MAKE US FEEL BETTER?

Meditation is not intended to make you feel better, but to enable you to be comfortable regardless of how you feel. Meditation is being awake, aware of what is happening.

When you study you may grasp certain things in principle. This knowledge may even have an immediate calming effect, but it is not yet stable or dependable.

To fully internalize your knowledge so that it becomes instinctive and second nature, you need to meditate. As you meditate you begin to appreciate experientially over and over again what you have learnt theoretically.

When you return to study the same things you will find you understand them differently because you have actually been there. You have experienced them deeply. This method of alternating study and meditation to internalize deeply is said to have originated from Nalanda University.[38]

DOES IT MATTER WHAT I DO IF IT ALL HAPPENS ANYWAY?

What you do matters very much. What you do influences many other people and things. What you do is also influenced by many other things. So you can imagine yourself at an intersection of an infinite multidimensional web of influences. You are influenced and in turn influence.

Your question comes from a different place, the belief that you are separate from the world. Find out what this thing you call "I" really is. What is it that is separate from the world and that can act independently of influences?

Ask yourself, "*Who* does what I do?" "*Who* operates this body and mind?" "Where is that?" Find the source and you will not find your question.

WHAT IS THE PLACE OF RESPONSIBILITY? ISN'T ALL THIS SHIRKING MY RESPONSIBILITIES?

Responsibility can be regarded as the *ability* to *respond* relevantly to what is happening. When you are aware of what

---

[38] Nalanda University: existed in Bihar, India from the fifth or sixth to the 12th century.

is really happening and can find no rational basis to discriminate between yourself and others, your natural desire to be happy and to avoid suffering will know no barriers and will apply itself to every situation without discrimination.

Do you believe in the concept of free will?

For me, my own particular opinions and beliefs are the results of my conditioning. Of course, this is also an opinion. People believe different things. You believe whatever you believe. Eliminating stress through being realistic does not involve specific beliefs but rather the appreciation that they are beliefs, ways of thinking about what is happening and not what is happening itself. This does not conflict with any belief as it does not adopt, identify with or reject any belief.

How do I apply this in everyday life?

There is absolutely nothing to apply. Understanding this is itself the application.

It is easy here with people that think like me.

In fact it is neither easy nor difficult. The error is trying to do something special. Whatever it is that you are trying to do, you say you find it easy here and difficult somewhere else. The only thing you can possibly do is what you are doing.

Can you possibly do something other than what you are doing? It is meaningless. So what effort do you need to expend in order to do what you are doing? How can it possibly be easy or difficult? There is no alternative.

Where is the place of planning in this method?

Planning happens as mental and physical activity. It is part of what happens. There is no need to relate to planning differently from the way you relate to any other activity. But it is useful to remember that because you are planning, that does not necessarily mean that what you plan will or will not happen. Then you will not be disappointed.

Plan happily, including any necessary contingency plans, but having done what you can, do not waste your precious time and energy worrying about the future.

Won't people take advantage of my compassion?

You yourself are the chief beneficiary of your compassion, which acts to remove mental stress. Compassion is relating to everyone and their difficulties equally, including of course yourself. This is a more comfortable way to live, regardless of how others respond to you.

Shouldn't we teach this to our children?

The form of work I am describing in this guide is suitable for adults. Children have different needs. However, to the extent that you mature through this work, your behavior with other people including children is likely to be more beneficial.

How do I know what is real and what is not?

Everything is real except for what you think. Reality is everything, but not the way you think it is. Ask yourself regularly, "What is this if not what I think?"

How can I be happy if I don't like who I am?

Who are you? What is this thing you claim you do not like? You yourself are not what you think. What you think you are is an opinion, a mental process. Who are you really then, apart from what you think you are? Find that out first. When you discover that you cannot find yourself other than your opinions, there will be nothing to like or dislike, so this will not create a barrier to your happiness.

Liking or not liking what you think you are, in addition to being meaningless, is an acquired habit learnt from your parents, teachers and the way your mind has interpreted what it thinks has happened to you through life over the years. Discover that historical habitual thinking pattern and you will find it dissolves without applying itself to what is happening now.

Can I be happy if my children are unhappy?

Definitely!

Quoted from a student who received this answer from a Tibetan lama in Katmandu. She knows who she is—thanks for this contribution.

I CAN DO IT HERE, BUT HOW DO I TAKE THIS WITH ME TO MY HOME AND WORK?

You have already absorbed what you can absorb. It is part of you and affects how you think, feel and behave. There is nothing to take home other than yourself.

Spend some quiet time every day with yourself to allow what you have absorbed to penetrate more deeply. Maintain regular contact with good teachers and spiritual, that is, realistic friends. That is all you need to do. The rest happens spontaneously.

MY COMPASSION MAKES ME SUFFER, KNOWING THERE IS SO MUCH SUFFERING IN THE WORLD. WHAT CAN I DO?

If you can do something useful, do it. Otherwise, keep your eyes, ears and heart open and go about your business.

I AM KIND TO OTHERS BUT THEY ARE NOT KIND TO ME. AM I A SUCKER?

When you are kind you benefit. When others are kind, they benefit. Other people's unkindness may cause you harm, but your own unkindness can destroy your peace of mind totally.

I LOOK AFTER OTHER PEOPLE BUT NOT AFTER MYSELF. HOW CAN I CHANGE THAT?

You only think you look after other people but not after yourself. You are probably building up a store of resentment which harms both you and others. You cannot possibly look after other people but not after yourself in practice because you are connected to, influenced by and influence other people in more ways than you can begin to understand.

The Buddha said that you can search the entire universe for someone who is more deserving of your love and affection than you are yourself, and that person is not to be found anywhere. You yourself, as much as anybody in the entire universe deserve your love and affection. Understand that you can find no rational basis for discrimination and you will treat all people equally including yourself. That is compassion.

You may ask, "If the 'I' isn't real, what about the 'you'?" It is said that the Buddha taught in 84,000 ways. In other words he matched his language to the questioner. As a result, he was not necessarily consistent in his language, but relevant.

WHAT DO BUDDHISTS MEAN BY "EMPTINESS"?

What you think is empty of real content. Your concepts are empty. They have no referent—they do not refer to anything except to themselves. Your thoughts do not bring you information about what is happening, but only about the magical games your mind plays. Even emptiness is empty of meaning—it refers to nothing at all so there is no need to concern yourself with it.

I HAVE BEEN TOLD THAT EVEN IF I GET UNCOMFORTABLE MEDITATING, I AM NOT ALLOWED TO MOVE. IS THIS TRUE?

Check whether you move in practice. Either you move or you do not. Meditation is being awake, present to whatever happens. Be present to your movement and to your absence of movement. That is meditation. It is impossible to meditate incorrectly. More precisely, the only way to meditate incorrectly is to try to meditate correctly.

Never try to do what you are told. Rather, be awake to what you actually do.

You can see that I am telling you here what to do, so that is also unnecessary.

I CANNOT MEDITATE. I AM ALWAYS THINKING. WHAT CAN I DO?

Meditation is not about stopping or starting thinking but about resting in awareness of whether a thought is or is not present at any moment.

IS MEDITATION TURNING INWARDS?

Find the wall between the inside and outside. When you fail to find the wall your question will have disappeared.

How do I disconnect from reality in order to meditate correctly?

Meditation is a family of techniques to *connect* you to reality. We are disconnected enough already—there is no need to increase that. Meditation is being awake, realistic. Most people are not realistic enough because they are occupied with what they think rather than what is. Meditation returns you to the real aspect of yourself.

Are you saying that I don't exist? I don't understand that!

I am saying neither that you exist nor that you do not exist. The question does not interest me. I am asking you to find out what the "I" is that does or does not exist. When you fail to find the "I" you are asking about, the question is also absent.

How long and how often should I meditate?

I recommend being in a meditative state, that is fully connected to and aware of what is actually happening, as much as possible. If you are looking for a meditation regime, start with five minutes two or three times a day. Listen to the sounds. Watch whatever you see. Notice your bodily sensations, breathing and thoughts.

I can't get rid of my thoughts

You cannot get rid of your breathing, blood stream or digestive system. How can you possibly get rid of your thoughts? Sit quietly, watch them and never forget they are just thoughts. Then, regardless of what thoughts occur, they cannot harm you.

Where is the place in this teaching for God or a moral belief system?

You believe in whatever you believe in. Meditation has nothing to do with beliefs, but with being awake, aware of your beliefs as beliefs, mental activities.

Acknowledgements

I first made contact with nondual meditation through meeting Dr. Peter Fenner, the Australian philosopher and Western nondual wisdom and psychotherapy pioneer and teacher. It was he who first distilled this work for me in the words, "Mental stress results from wanting a reality different from what it is." I deeply appreciate his presence, generosity and embodiment of deep and rigorous understanding and expression.

I was fortunate to have had the opportunity of a personal retreat at the Dzogchen Monastery in India and revealing conversations with the Seventh Dzogchen Rinpoche, Jigme Losel Wangpo.

Through them I was introduced to the work and lives of masters of major Buddhist and other nondual traditions including Dzogchen, Mahamudra, Zen, Madhyamika, Advaita and Tao. These remain the primary sources of inspiration for this guide, my teaching and my personal practice.

I have been inspired by many other sources also, such as the teachings of Krishnamurti, Ramana Maharshi, Nisargadatta Maharaj, Alan Watts, Albert Einstein and Wilfred Bion.

Thanks to Barbara Grant for all the time and energy invested in her voluntary detailed and sensitive language and content editing, both of which have contributed greatly to the quality of the work

My thanks to Ira Keren who voluntarily designed the book and nursed all the editions through the many cover and content design and typesetting processes.

I am very grateful for the help and inspiration of many students, teachers, friends and family who have helped, inspired and encouraged me both to create and to improve this guide.

REFERENCES

Lao Tzu. Tao Te Ching. translated by Gia-Fu Feng and Jane English. New York, NY: Random House, 1972.

Joshu. Radical Zen: The Sayings of Joshu. translated and commentated by Yoel Hoffman. Brookline, MA: Autumn Press, 1978.

Longchen Rabjam. The Precious Treasury of the Way of Abiding. translated by Richard Barron (Chökyi Nyima). Junction City, CA: Padma, 1998.

Suzuki, D.T. Essays in Zen Buddhism. London: Rider, 1953.

Afterword

I feel I have been looking for "the truth," for happiness and release from mental tension, for an indefinite period. I am aware of many stages of searching, starting with an amorphous childhood longing for peace from a troubled background, through more or less structured attempts at self-examination, science, religion, psychotherapy, nondual Buddhist training, meditation and teaching.

To begin to discover and even appreciate deep down that the whole search was, in a sense, unnecessary, that, as the Buddha said, "there is no need to seek the truth; it is enough to abandon your opinions," was a great relief to me.

I hope this guide has given you some useful tools to guide you to live better.

I wish you success in finding what you want.

I wish you fulfillment of all your desires.

Beyond that, I wish you unconditional peace of mind and happiness independently of whether or not you get what you want.

Good luck!

Jonathan Harrison

A Reminder

You are unlikely to acquire your desired result from this or other books alone. Although you can gain valuable information and inspiration from books, only a realized teacher or friend can help you gain the extremely subtle appreciation of the truth.

You feel something special in the presence of a realized teacher that lends context and deep cognitive and experiential resonance to other, passive, sources of information. All the traditions emphasize the essential role of direct transmission between teacher and student.

This guide is not intended to replace teachers but to be used, together with study with a teacher and regular meditation, as a handbook, to clarify and to act as a reminder.

Allocation of specific times to relax and allow meditation to occur is a good idea, but also a habit. For this we usually need a teacher and other friends with the same idea. They support us until the habit is stable.

Resources

Here are some books and online resources dealing with nondual understanding:

Online

http://www.radiantmind.net – the website of Peter Fenner

http://www.youtube.com/watch?v=6VQDcIO3PVI – "The Flame of Being": Jean Klein interviewed by Michael Toms. Santa Barbara, CA: Third Millennium, 1989 (excerpt)

http://www.sriramanamaharshi.org – website dedicated to the teachings of Ramana Maharshi

http://www.youtube.com/watch?v=DaJwuhs0ZPM –video talk by the Dzogchen master Chögyal Namkhai Norbu

Books

Fenner, Peter. Radiant Mind: Awakening Unconditioned Awareness. Boulder, CO: Sounds Truc, 2007.

Longchen Rabjam. The Precious Treasury of the Way of Abiding. translated by Richard Barron (Chökyi Nyima). Junction City, CA: Padma, 1998.

Ramana Maharshi. Be As You Are. edited by David Godman. London: Arkana, 1985.

Watts, Alan W. The Way of Zen. New York, NY: Pantheon, 1957.

Nisargadatta Maharaj. The Ultimate Medicine. edited by Robert Powell. San Diego, CA: Blue Dove Press, 1994.

You can find more recommendations in the bibliography at my website: https://endingstress.org/reading-suggestions/.

HOW TO CONTACT ME

I teach worldwide by video and voice calls.

You are welcome to contact me and I will respond as soon as I can.

You can find my contact details at my website https://endingstress.org/contact. If you would like to receive regular teachings from me, you can subscribe there also.

INDEX

anger, v, 7, 12, 51, 52, 54, 56, 57, 71, 85, 147

anxiety, 1, 7, 12, 45, 46, 47, 49, 92, 96, 106, 129, 141

apathy, 146

Avalokiteshvara, 120

beliefs, 14

bodhisattva, 120

buddhism, 5, 13, 17, 19, 28, 38, 61, 75, 93, 117, 120, 161

concepts, 7, 13, 30, 31, 32, 35, 46, 66, 81, 91, 145, 155

conditioned mind, 49

conflict, 81

constructs, 31, 32, 46, 60, 64, 120, 130

crisis, 24, 113

Dalai Lama, 13, 28, 56, 89, 93, 127

death, 24, 34, 49, 77, 93, 96, 105, 110, 120

decisions, 24, 75, 76, 77, 79, 80, 82, 110

disappointment, 12, 71

dualistic, 5, 13, 14, 146

Dzogchen, 7, 17, 20, 61, 127, 159, 167

envy, 12

expectations, 15, 16, 26, 32, 47, 49, 53, 69, 70, 71, 72, 73, 130, 139

facts, 3, 13, 14, 48, 96, 140

fear, v, 7, 12, 45, 46, 85, 93

fixations, 32, 59, 60

free will, 151

frustration, 12, 17, 27, 51, 57

hope, 8, 40, 45, 46, 163

ideas, 14, 32, 46, 91, 142

INDEX

illness, 24, 28, 66

illusion, 17, 18, 45, 101, 143

insight meditation, 62, 70, 111, 129, 130, 131

Joshu, 117, 118, 161

kindness, 27, 89, 92, 93

Krishnamurti, 23, 51, 95, 109, 111, 127, 159

Longchen Rabjam, 17, 118, 143, 161, 167

love, 17, 24, 25, 26, 27, 42, 43, 60, 92, 93, 95, 119, 126, 133, 146, 148, 155

Mahamudra, 7, 61, 134, 159

Mahatma Gandhi, 148

Mahayana, 5, 19, 38, 120

meditation, v, 2, 7, 8, 17, 20, 21, 22, 25, 27, 48, 57, 61, 66, 67, 72, 90, 95, 107, 109, 111, 114, 121, 125, 126, 127, 129, 130, 131, 133, 134, 135, 143, 145, 146, 148, 149, 150, 156, 157, 159, 163, 165

mental stress, 11, 65, 159

mind, vii, 1, 5, 12, 13, 14, 15, 17, 18, 21, 23, 30, 32, 33, 34, 46, 48, 49, 60, 61, 62, 66, 67, 76, 81, 82, 83, 88, 89, 90, 107, 110, 111, 114, 115, 118, 119, 130, 131, 133, 134, 138, 140, 141, 142, 143, 150, 153, 154, 155, 163

morality, 148, 149

Nagarjuna, 19, 59

natural awareness, 7, 17, 18, 22, 62

nondual, v, 5, 6, 7, 55, 86, 120, 145, 146, 159, 167

non-meditation, 131

opinions, 13, 14, 15, 31, 48, 54, 63, 66, 85, 90, 96, 97, 98, 99, 112, 139, 151, 153, 163

pain, 3, 29, 30, 65, 66, 67, 93, 119

prajnaparamita, 5, 120

reality, 2, 5, 7, 11, 12, 14, 15, 17, 18, 21, 31, 32, 33, 40, 46, 48, 49, 51, 52, 53, 54, 61, 69, 70, 71, 72, 80, 81, 83, 85, 90, 95, 99, 106, 116, 125, 126, 129, 130, 135, 146, 157, 159

religion, 13, 23, 55, 89, 93, 163

security, 45, 46, 102

self-criticism, 60

shamatha, 129

stress, iii, v, vii, 2, 3, 7, 8, 11, 12, 14, 15, 16, 18, 20, 24, 27, 29, 46, 48, 56, 65, 66, 67, 77, 79, 80, 82, 89, 90, 116, 117, 147, 151, 152

structures, 13, 14, 32, 63, 86, 120, 130

suffering, 5, 28, 29, 30, 65, 67, 107, 119, 120, 146, 147, 151, 154

Sutralamkara, 12

tension, 12, 65, 67, 70, 89, 145, 163

thoughts, 11, 14, 15, 16, 17, 18, 21, 22, 30, 31, 32, 34, 35, 39, 40, 46, 47, 48, 52, 53, 54, 59, 61, 62, 63, 68, 70, 72, 76, 82, 83, 85, 86, 90, 91, 92, 94, 95, 109, 111, 112, 120, 126, 127, 129, 130, 131, 139, 140, 141, 142, 145, 147, 155, 157, 158

uncertainty, 45, 46, 47, 48, 50, 60, 82

unconditioned mind, 49

vipashyana, 129, 130

worry, v, 7, 12, 37, 38, 39, 75, 79, 109

Made in the USA
Las Vegas, NV
18 May 2021